Building Your Play

Building Your Play

Theory and Practice for the Beginning Playwright

David Rush

Southern Illinois University Press / Carbondale and Edwardsville

13   12   11   10   4   3   2   1

Library of Congress Cataloging-in-Publication Data
Rush, David, date.
Building your play : theory and practice for the begin-
ning playwright / David Rush.
    p. cm.
 Includes index.
ISBN-13: 978-0-8093-2959-5 (alk. paper)
ISBN-10: 0-8093-2959-X (alk. paper)
ISBN-13: 978-0-8093-8582-9 (ebook)
ISBN-10: 0-8093-8582-1 (ebook)
 1. Drama—Technique. 2. Playwriting. I. Title.
 PN1661.R87 2010
 808.2—dc22   2009045986

Thanks to my students, who taught me everything I know

Contents

Acknowledgments

Many voices are heard in this book besides mine, and more hands than my two have gone into shaping it. Kristine Priddy at Southern Illinois University Press made it happen. John Wilson made it better. Wayne Larsen made it easy. And a couple dozen professionals through whose critical eyes the manuscript passed have made it usable.

Many thanks to all.

Building Your Play

Introduction

Before we start, I want to lay out some of the assumptions and premises on which this book is based. There are several playwriting books out there, and each has something different to offer you. What's this one all about?

To begin with, this book is primarily designed for the beginning playwright, somebody who has probably been in a few plays, has worked backstage once or twice, reads plays, and in general loves theater. Perhaps you are in a course at school, or perhaps you saw a production of a play that inspired you, or perhaps it's something you always wanted to try and are now about to. Therefore, this book will introduce you to some very basic ideas, concepts, and techniques. Think of it as Playwriting 101.

However, it can be useful for advanced writers as well—those of you who may already be familiar with some of this material. You may have a command of the ideas and concepts, although you may know them by different terms. In that case, you will find this a great refresher for you; it can be a way to reconnect with some of those elementary steps that we often forget are extremely important. If you're having second (or third) draft problems, it's very useful to step back, remind yourself of the basics, and see where you've made some elementary mistakes. Think of it as baking a cake. The beginner needs to know the difference between, say, a tablespoon and a teaspoon. The advanced baker knows the difference, but when the cake turns out flat, she needs to go back to the recipe and make sure she's used the right measure. It's always smart to begin at the beginning.

How Does the Book Work?

Some people assume that teaching playwriting is very much like dissecting a frog or analyzing a joke. The problem with that approach is that a living frog or a successful joke depends on everything working right all at the same time. Once you remove the heart, the frog ceases to be a frog and becomes a corpse. Once you stop to explain why a joke is funny, it instantly stops being funny. Similarly, a play only works when all of its parts are unified—every scene, every strategy, every goal, every physical activity and line of dialogue—when all of these components support each other. For instance, in chapter 6, I make the point that a *plot* is composed of a series of scenes and moments that the writer has chosen for a sound reason. Out of all the possible things that can happen to a character, or that a character might choose to do, the writer has put some things in and left some things out. Why? Because including only the right scenes will illuminate one of the characters the writer is creating. The principle is that we learn who people are because of the things they say and do. Consider two men who want to get rich quickly. One decides to spend his last dollar on a lottery ticket, while the other decides to rob a bank. In each case, the action has defined the person. Therefore, while the chapter is dealing with plot per se, it's also indirectly dealing with character, with rhythm, with theme, and with a host of other ideas. Like the parts of a frog, they all work together.

So, as you proceed, you may find yourself wandering around the trees and forgetting about the forest. But that's all right. It's perfectly fine to get lost for a while. After all, that's what second drafts are for.

How Is the Book Arranged?

A second assumption that underlies this book is manifest in the arrangement and content of its chapters. It approaches the craft of playwriting from a mixed point of view. On the one hand, there's quite a bit of dramatic theory involved: defining terms, discussing critical precepts, and generally talking about a play in an abstract sense. These sections are then followed by some very practical "How-to" passages, operating in some ways like a recipe book for making a cake. So you'll find out as you work your way through it, not just *how* to write a play, but *what* exactly it is that you're trying to write at all. Hopefully, you'll come away from your time with the book understanding not just *what* do to, but *why* you're doing it.

Thus, each chapter first explains a concept and then provides some specific writing exercises to give you practice in putting that concept to work. You'll also find that each chapter ends with some discussion of rewrites. This is for future reference: as you continue to write plays, you will find yourself meeting a wide variety of problems along the way. People will respond to your work with questions that, after a time, will become familiar to you. You can use these questions to guide you as you figure out what to fix and how to fix it.

You'll also find that the book provides many examples of what other writers have done with problems similar to those you encounter. And you will note that most of the examples come primarily from two plays. I believe it's more useful to examine a couple of plays in great detail rather than many plays on a superficial level. Because all parts of a play are inextricably joined together, you need to see how the various elements we will be discussing work in relation to all the others and to the whole. Thus we'll be looking extensively at both *Othello* by William Shakespeare and *The Glass Menagerie* by Tennessee Williams.

In addition to these two primary sources, however, I occasionally draw examples from other important dramas. Although you might not be familiar with these other plays, I think the examples should be self-explanatory. Furthermore, I hope you'll be encouraged to read them and become familiar with some major classics. You can never read too many plays.

Looking at the book as a whole, you'll note that it is divided into three distinct sections.

Part One: The Fundamentals

This section teaches you the fundamentals of all drama, the four building blocks, if you will, that form the structure of almost every play you will read or write. As we'll examine in great detail in the individual chapters, the first and foremost element of every play is *action*—that is, somebody doing something. Action is the essence of every moment in the work, as atoms are the essence of every element in nature. Although we'll go into greater detail on this later, for now it's enough to realize that an action always consists of four things working together. Everything that happens in a play is about (1) somebody who (2) wants to achieve something, which (3) for one reason or another is difficult to achieve, and thus (4) will do whatever it takes to achieve it. The chapters in this section explain these in detail. In other words, if you think of a play as a house, you're learning to make bricks.

Part Two: Putting Them Together

This section teaches you how best to use the fundamentals to craft plays that are interesting, clear, and effective. You'll learn about how to put scenes together in a coherent and meaningful order, how to generate suspense as your play progresses, how to keep your individual scenes from becoming static, confusing, and—the worst sin of all—boring. You'll learn how to put the bricks together to make that house.

Part Three: Some Advanced Tricks

This section teaches you some useful tools to further sharpen, deepen, and focus your work. It is here that you'll learn more about dialogue, characterization, exposition, and other matters. Please note: other books and teachers may consider some of what I call "advanced tricks" to be "basic." They will claim that you have to begin with "character" first—let the audience know who the people are! To my mind, however, character cannot exist independent of action. As I mentioned above, and as I'll mention again below—the point can't be stressed too often—people only know about other people because of what they see and hear them do. Character may *cause* action, but, in plays, it's *action* that reveals character. Thus, to my mind, action comes first. Sounds a little complicated and overwhelming? Don't worry. It'll all make sense as we go step by step through the process.

Two Important Cautions

In my teaching experience, I have learned that beginning playwrights often make some of the same mistakes when they get started. Let me lay them out here as overall cautions, something to keep in the back of your mind as you work through the chapters.

1. A Play Is Not a Novel, a Short Story, or a Screenplay

A play is a text designed to be performed live by actors on a stage, presented live to an audience in the same room. This sounds very obvious and almost silly, but it does imply several important restrictions.

You are limited in what you can do

Fiction has the advantage of coming alive only in the reader's imagination: there are no physical limitations on what can be shown or described. You can write "a large army crosses the river" and let readers conjure up any image they want. Film has the advantage of being created by cameras and editing—increasingly with the aid of computers and limited only by the budget the producer allows. Thus, you can shoot an army on the march, a long shot of a river, the weary expressions on soldiers' faces, and so forth. You can edit all these shots into a sequence that shows the excitement, horror, tension, and emotion of a battle. The audience watching the film never moves.

By contrast, since plays are performed live, you cannot create elaborate effects; you cannot easily jump from one set to another, or have a character wearing a red dress one second and a blue suit of armor the next. One of the most common glitches in stage directions is when a playwright states something like, "*She leaves the stage. A moment later, she comes back wearing a big hat.*" Try to visualize this. After the actress has left the stage, what happens on stage during that "moment"? Do the other characters stand there and wait for her? Is there a thirty-second pause? Can you imagine how deadly dull thirty seconds of nothing could be? In other words, you have to allow for the limits of time, space, and technical facilities and visualize what the audience will actually be watching.

Remember: Audiences can only understand
what they are able to see or hear

Fiction can take us inside the thoughts of a character. You can write, "George was afraid of heights," and the reader will understand. However, the only way a theater audience can know of George's fear is by seeing or hearing something that physically communicates this fear. You must create some activity or some line that reveals this. How? What can George (or somebody else) do or say that does this?

Again, at first glance, this also seems obvious, but you would be surprised how many beginning playwrights write extensive stage directions that say things like "As George goes to the window, he wonders whether he'll be able to open it. His fear of heights begins to affect him and he thinks he might cry." Since an audience can't get inside George's head, you need to physicalize this. This, essentially, is another way of saying—and stressing—what was mentioned above: the building block of all plays is *action*.

Please keep these restrictions in mind. As we study various specific parts of playwriting, these factors will be very important.

2. Plays Come in Many Shapes and Sizes

As we work our way through this book, you'll eventually learn how to write what is typically called a conventional "well-made play"; that is, a fairly realistic play about more or less recognizable people saying and doing more or less recognizable things. Nearly all plays you study or see will be of this type.

However, this is not the only kind of play that exists. There are many other works out there that call themselves plays that don't follow these rules at all. Think of a play as you would a painting. Some paintings are very realistic: you look at them and see something as it might exist in your own world. If it's an image of people on a beach, they look like people, the beach looks like a beach, the water looks like water, and the beverages they are guzzling look very appetizing. However, some paintings are not that at all. Examine the work of any number of modern artists such as Picasso, Klee, Rauschenberg, Pollock, and others, and what do you see? Shapes, squiggles, lines, and masses; people with both eyes on the same side of their heads, a collage of images all pasted together, and who knows what. There's nothing resembling reality at all.

But are you sure? Perhaps the "reality" the artist is painting is not the reality on the surface of things, but a sort of interior reality that exists underneath. Or perhaps it's a subjective reality: we are seeing the world not through our own eyes, but through the eyes of the artist: a painting might not be an objective image of a real woman at all, but the *idea* of a woman as the artist perceives her. In other words, there are all kinds of ways to paint reality.

Plays are similar. Most plays with which you are familiar try to reflect reality in a way that, well, looks "real." The characters are supposed to look like, speak like, and behave like people would "normally" do; the events that occur are supposed to follow the "normal" laws of logic, causality, and appearance. Things happen one after another; something causes something else; events lead to a climax, and something changes; we find ourselves watching a story that has a beginning, middle, and end, as though a slice of life were cut from the world and pasted onto a stage for us to examine.

However, again, not all plays are meant to be stories. Some plays do not show us things in linear time, but rather in a distorted sequence, in which we see the end before we see the beginning and work backwards. Not all plays follow the laws of logic: because Event "A" happens *before* Event "B" does not mean that "A" *causes* "B"—after all, day comes before night, but day does not *cause* night. Not all the people we see on stage are meant to be lifelike characters, such as we might meet on the street. Sometimes the figures are abstractions of concepts—for example, in the medieval play *Everyman,* you meet "Good Deeds," "Fellowship," "Kindred and Kin," and so forth. They are symbolic of ideas and thus don't have to behave as living people do.

Furthermore, not all plays have to show us events at all. Sometimes what we see and hear from the stage sounds like gibberish—as though the writer were playing with sounds and words in the haphazard fashion of jazz. Sometimes the actors do weird things that make no sense: Why, for instance, does this woman come riding on the stage in a bathtub singing the national anthem, throw a rotten egg onto the floor, and ride off? Especially when we thought we were out in a field at midnight? Take a look at a collage such as those created by Bob Rauschenberg (Google him on your browser): sometimes plays are like that.

Nevertheless, as we said, most of the plays that you know or want to write are of the familiar, so-called real style. They are traditional, they are well-made (in the sense of following the rules of normality), and they are easily accessible—we can understand them. These are the kinds of plays that this manual is talking about, plays that follow certain laws in order to create meaningful experiences for their audiences. We will be concerned with what *these* laws are. In other words, this book will teach you how to write a traditional, well-made play. There may come a time when you don't want to write that kind of play; but that's the subject for another book. Pick up a copy of Paul Castagno's excellent work on that subject, *New Playwriting Strategies: A Language Based Approach to Playwriting* (Routledge, 2001).

3. You Are a Beginner and Are Bound to Do Some Foolish Things

Writing is always a dangerous task. We put on the page our private thoughts and desires and invest an awful lot of our egos in the work. So, when the work is inferior, the characters dead, the dialogue awful, the whole thing confusing and inept—we tend to feel bad. Embarrassed. Discouraged. Awful. I've been there myself, and I know.

But remember, you are a *beginner.* You didn't start off ice skating by doing triple turns: you started off by learning how to fall. You didn't win the first chess game you played: you were trounced mercilessly. Learning to write is the same way: You are here first to make mistakes, to write bad scenes, to create deadly dull characters, and then learn how to avoid or to fix them. That's why they call it "school."

So allow yourself the freedom and luxury to write awful stuff. Take advantage of the safety of the classroom and in knowing that we're all in this together and we've all been there. Write whatever you're capable of and as much of it as you can. Get it out of your system. You'll come out the other end a much better writer after all. Just keep these basic parameters in mind:

- A play is not a novel or film.
- We are concerned here with only one form of play: the traditional, well-made kind.
- You are here to experiment, to write stuff you'll later look back on as garbage. You are learning. You will write the great stuff later.

So, enough of the preliminaries. Turn the page and let's get started.

Part One

The Fundamentals

1

Is It a Play?

Where do we begin? The first thing we need to do is understand what exactly it is we're creating here. We're not creating a novel, a film, a painting, a poem, or even a short story. A play is a unique art form and has important features. So where do you start? You can start in any number of places. You know an interesting story you think would be stageworthy. You know a weird and complex person you think might make a good character. You feel strongly about a social issue and want to change the body politic. Or you had a bizarre dream last night you want to translate to the stage. However, as intriguing as these brain-seeds might be, not all of them have the potential to be a play. So, let's start by defining what a play is and note how it differs from other forms of storytelling.

An Operating Definition

We can begin by defining a play as "something that happens to a person." A good start, but not everything that happens to a person has the makings of a drama. We need something more specific.

It might be useful as a beginning to point out that a play is not the same thing as a story. A play may (and often does) contain within it a story, but not every story can make a play. I can best explain this by borrowing from a work by Henry James called *The Art of Fiction* and elaborating a little on his theory. Suppose I tell you the following two statements:

1. The king died.
2. The queen died.

What do I have? I have a collection of *facts*. Two things happened. True. But that's all. Now, suppose I gave you these two statements:

1. The king died.
2. Two weeks later, the queen died.

What do I have now? I have *history;* that is, a chronological sequence of events in which one follows another in time. Now, suppose I give you these two statements:

1. The king died.
2. Two weeks later, the queen died of grief.

What do I have now? Now I have, at last, a *story;* that is, a series of events that are causally connected and that, as a whole, relate a larger event that has coherence and meaning. So there's a story involved here: of two people, royalty, who are so much in love that even death won't separate them. But now, suppose I give you this statement:

"Guess what? The cook told me that the upstairs maid told her that the butler found the queen hanging from her chandelier with a note attached to her big toe that said, 'I cannot live without Henry, and I'm going to join him!'"

Now what do I have? I have the way in which the story is communicated. How the story is told. In what form it is revealed to the audience. And this last statement is the one that makes the play. In other words, a play is *a form of communication (or art) in which a story is revealed.*

In this case, the play would consist of a dialogue between two people: say, a footman who speaks the above line and a butler who listens. The play itself concerns the relationship between the footman and the butler, the reasons the footman tells the story, and other interesting angles, but the story of the king and queen gets told. Of course, there might be other ways to tell the same story—other sorts of "plays." The story might be told to us by a news anchor on the ten o'clock news, in which case the play concerns the anchor and his or her reading. Or the story might be told to us by somebody who reads to somebody else the long, last letter the queen actually wrote, and the play concerns the reader and the reader's audience. Or the story might be told to us directly; that is, we might actually see the events take place in front of us: the queen nursing the sick man, his death and burial, her despair, her writing the note, tying the rope, and jumping off the table. In this case, the play concerns the story directly. Can you think of other ways in which the story could be communicated?

Thus, a story is "What happened." The play is "How do we get told?"

The matter gets a little more complicated, however. There are certain kinds of stories that make for good plays, and some that don't. There are certain conventions and forms that plays have that lend themselves to good stories. Let's take a look at what this means. Let's take a closer look at what makes a *play* and how it tells its story.

Take a look at Little Red Riding Hood, for example. She is born, grows up, goes to school, dates a jock, loses her parents, and goes to live with her stepmom, who sends her into the forest to bring cookies to Grandma. She meets a wolf, goes on her way, and has a big shock when she gets to Grandma's house. After that, she marries a woodsman, goes to live in France, and writes several best-selling cookbooks. She contracts a rare form of cancer and dies peacefully in her sleep one summer night.

Lots of things are happening here in her life. But do any of them contain within themselves the qualities that make a potential play? A lot of things may happen in your draft, but do they add up to some one important, significant event that forms a dramatic action? Something that has shape, coherence, and meaning?

In order to find out, let's lay down a definition that will guide us and then apply it to Red's situation. Let's agree on this:

A play is a specific event that takes place over a finite unit of time in which a significant change takes place either within a central character, or a larger situation, or both.

Let's take the key components one at a time.

Key Components

1. A Specific Event

By this, we mean that one particular thing happens. Something takes place, something is done. However, we can label that "thing" in a variety of ways. The thing can be very small, such as "Red visits Grandma," or "Red writes a school book report." Or the thing can be considered on a larger scale, as in "Red becomes president of Woodsville," or "Red learns the meaning of life."

The thing may be self-contained, as in "Red picks roses," or it may contain within it several smaller "things," such as "Red picks up her shears. Red puts on her gardening clothes. Red goes outside. Red finds a basket. Red cuts five roses off the bush." You can certainly look at each of these small steps as an individual event in itself, but you can also look at them collectively and use the *total* of what they do to define our specific event.

Look at Red's life as we outlined it above. Her whole life could be seen as one event: Red's Slow Journey to Death (depressing, but true). Or a section of it can be seen as one event (even though that section may contain several happenings): Red goes through high school; Red grows up; Red marries the woodsman; Red journeys to France; Red becomes a best-selling author.

Now, take *Othello*. The play is filled with happenings, each one of them a sort of "event" in itself. Othello marries Desdemona. Desdemona's father tries to get her back. Iago gets Cassio drunk. Roderigo threatens Iago, and later Iago kills Roderigo. Desdemona and Othello quarrel over a handkerchief. Othello murders his wife. Othello kills himself. Lots of things happen, but is there one event that the entire play shows us? Is there one thing that it all adds up to? Sure. "Iago destroys Othello." Or to put it another way, "Iago gets Othello to kill himself," an event that takes the whole play to complete.

Thus, a specific event is a one-thing-that-happens, considered on both a large and small scale. Playwrights often use the terms *action* or *dramatic action* to mean this same concept. I like the term *overall dramatic action* since it suggests that the whole play is concerned with this event.

An exercise

Look at *The Glass Menagerie*. Each individual scene is an event in itself: Amanda and Tom quarrel. Amanda tries to earn a living. Amanda chastises Laura. What events do you find in the rest of the scenes? What one event takes place over the whole play? Some possible answers:

- Amanda understands something
- Tom leaves
- Laura becomes crushed

Your choice?

2. A Finite Unit of Time

This means borders. We've already hinted at this concept in the section above, when we had to decide on the scope of our event. But whether it's on a large scale or a small scale, observe that this event starts at some particular point in time and then ends at another particular point in time. It doesn't go on forever; it can't. A quick look at the examples from Red's life should make this clear. There is a time, for instance, when she's in the house and thinking about flowers and decides to go pick some roses. Then, after a while, there is another time when she's back in the house and has a bunch of roses in her hand. It's the section of time between those two situations that we're looking at; the time in which Red "picks roses." This is the event, nicely defined by a starting point and a stopping point.

3. A Significant Change Occurs

This is the most important ingredient of all. It simply alerts us to the fact that the event has made an important difference to somebody in some way. After it's all over, things are not the same. Somebody has grown, perhaps, or died, or learned some valuable lesson, or seen the world in a new way. Red was single; now she's married. Red was innocent; now she's wise. Red was alive; now she's dead. Indeed, you might consider the word *change* to be the single most important word in all of playwriting.

Writers often refer to this process of change as the "arc" of the play; it's that overall controlling idea that permeates the various scenes and leads us from one condition to another. Furthermore, we often describe this arc by using a verb plus a complement or a modifier (i.e., a predicate phrase). If you look back at the paragraphs above, you'll note that this is always the case: for example, "grows up," "goes through high school," "takes vengeance," and so forth.

This element of change can happen on several levels. Let's take them up one at a time. Often, a play will have more than one of them working simultaneously.

Physical

In the most basic sense, a character's physical situation changes. This may involve geography: she may begin in Chicago and end up in New York, but it may have taken her an entire life of struggle to get there. Another character's health might change: he may begin with a life-threatening disease and end up being cured. Or he might start out alive and end up dead. *The Glass Menagerie,* for example, is on one level a play about a large physical change: Tom begins in St. Louis and ends up in some strange, unnamed city. Or we might say Tom starts out inside the apartment and ends up outside. What would be a predicate phrase that expresses the change? "Leaving home."

Keep in mind that physical acts involve small things as well as large: Speaking up after a period of silence is a physical act, as is speaking one word instead of another, or sitting down after standing. Can you imagine a whole play devoted to the process of "standing up"? Certainly, if it begins with Jeff as an invalid with polio, unable to walk, and ends with Jeff taking his first step. Can you imagine a whole play devoted to "walking out the door"? Read a little further.

Mental

But, of course, physical acts don't take place in isolation. They are accompanied by other kinds of activities. Here's the first: A character may achieve some important new way of looking at the world, beginning the play in ignorance or naiveté and ending the play in wisdom or experience. The mind has expanded and come to a new place. This can happen in two ways.

1. *A character has a major insight into something.* In *The Glass Menagerie,* Tom, in his final speech, tells us that he now understands the world; it is "lit by lightning." He's become wise. What's the predicate phrase for that? "Discovering a truth about the world."

2. *A character finally makes a major decision.* Tom has had enough and finally leaves home. Hamlet finally decides to actually *do* what he's been charged to do. Often the decision is a result of something learned; Macbeth decides to face Macduff because he's learned that life is but "a walking shadow / A tale told by an idiot." What's predicate phrase expresses this? "Deciding to die."

Social

The nature of a character's relations with others changes. Othello starts out as a respected general; at the end he's a deceived villain who has ruined not only his reputation but his life. Tom begins as part of the family; then he becomes a runaway. In every romantic comedy, the nature of the social change is obvious: somebody is single, and then they're married. What are some predicate phrases that express the changes? "Punishing himself," "Leaving home," and "Getting married."

Symbolic

Of course, while we can look at plays as dramatizing the above kinds of changes, we are always aware that the play in question is at bottom often about something a little larger. Certainly Tom makes a decision, leaves the apartment, and removes himself from the family. But there's something deeper going on. We might say Tom is escaping his conventional life, or that Tom is destroying his illusions, or that Tom is growing up mentally and emotionally. Some would say that, in a way, *The Glass Menagerie* is all about "Tom coming out of the closet." We can apply this larger, symbolic lens to almost any play and see that its physical, mental, and social changes have greater resonance. Thus, as we've seen above, Othello goes from being beloved and honored to ending up a pariah who needs to be killed. But what's the larger implication of it all? Perhaps Othello also "loses his illusions."

As you've no doubt seen already, every play deals with changes on many levels all at the same time, depending on how you interpret the play. This is very useful for students of literature and scholars writing dissertations. But how does this affect you as a playwright? Simply put, while your play may be all about these many symbolic things, you can not write them all. Nor can the audience perceive them all. You can only operate on one of these levels. Which one?

The physical, of course.

You've read this a few pages back: The audience only knows what it can see or what it can hear. It watches as the character stands or sits, shoots or puts the gun away, kisses or hits the girl, goes to the chair or out the door. It listens as the character talks about her fears, tells her mother she's going to get married, confesses to the priest her previous sins, or announces that she's going to Cleveland after all.

Which means that your job as a playwright is to find the physical act (moving in some way or speaking one thing as opposed to another.) that conveys the idea of the others. In other words, you cannot write a play about a character achieving wisdom, but you can write a play about a character walking out of a house. (It happens in *The Glass Menagerie;* it also happens in *A Doll's House.*) You cannot write a play about a character understanding the universe, but you can write a play about a character asking dozens of people about his past until he hears the real truth. (It happens in *Oedipus;* it also happens in *The Importance of Being Earnest.*) You cannot write a play about a woman becoming isolated from society, but you can write a play about a woman committing suicide. (It happens in *Hedda Gabbler, 'Night, Mother,* and others.) The challenge is to create the physical manifestation of something going on much deeper. We'll come back to this point a little later on, when we talk about goals.

Caveat

This opening chapter throws a heavy dose of theory at you all at once. It may sound a bit overwhelming. And you may not have all the answers at once. You may sense that your character undergoes a physical change but not really know what it means. Or you may fully understand what sort of mental growth takes place but haven't quite found the physical equivalence of it.

Don't worry. Remember that writing your early draft is a process of discovery for you: you will explore different possibilities, see what works and what doesn't, and make whatever changes along they way you need to. But now that you know what you're looking for, you'll have a better chance of finding it.

Exercise 1:1

Choose one of the following plays and describe the nature of the change in each on all four levels:

> *Oedipus Rex*
> *Hamlet*
> *Trifles*
> *A Doll's House*
> *Fences*
> *Miss Julie*
> *Our Town*
> *Death of a Salesman*

Exercise 1:2

Here are matched sets of lines—supposedly the first and last lines of a play. In each case, there is some important change that has occurred. Write the verb or predicate phrase that best describes that change. Consider all four levels in your answer.

I can't move my legs!	I actually walked to the refrigerator!
Should I marry Tom Jones or Harry Smith?	Call me Mrs. Smith!
Look at those lovely flowers outside.	Look at the flowers I picked for you.
I wish I knew how to write a play!	I want to accept this award as best playwright of the year by thanking my first teacher.

Exercise 1:3

Here are several predicate phrases that describe changes that might occur in a play. In the reverse of the previous exercise, write a first and last line for that play:

1. Getting divorced.
2. Getting teacher to change grade.
3. Growing wiser.
4. Overcoming a fear.
5. Leaving home.

Revision Questions

As you develop plays in the future, you may hear responses to your early drafts that include comments such as these:

> It didn't seem to hang together for me.
> It didn't seem to end; it just seemed to stop.
> I couldn't figure out what it was all about; it seemed to wander.
> What was I supposed to get from the ending? It didn't relate or make sense.

Responses of this sort suggest that your first step is confusing: you haven't focused on one central action. For future reference, ask yourself these questions of any play you write:

1. Can you describe what happens in your play as *one* event? What significant difference is there between the beginning and the ending? Can the audience identify and understand what that difference is?

2. Similarly, is there an important change that occurs within your central character? How is he or she different at the end of the play than at the beginning?

3. How has this change operated on each of the four levels? Is one more important than the others?

4. Have you been able to find a physical act that embodies the others? If the audience were only to *see* or *hear* your character do or say *one* thing—which would somehow communicate the idea of the play—what might that be?

2

The Four Keys

You're pretty sure what you have is a play: It's an event that starts someplace and ends someplace different, and there is definitely a change involved. Good start: you've created a box; you have a situation you can work with. Now we need to understand how to fill it; how to make this event interesting, compelling, and meaningful. After all, when Red Riding Hood goes outside to pick a handful of roses, she's theoretically completed an action, and that could be a play. However, it's easy to see that just this alone is boring and meaningless. We need to add elements to this basic event to make it what we shall call *dramatic*. We need to examine the *four keys*.

What Are the Four Keys?

Let's revisit our definition of a play and examine the nature of the event itself. Let's now add this:

> An event becomes dramatic when it involves somebody who urgently wants something that is hard to get and does whatever is necessary to get it.

Note that this definition carefully contains four key elements. Let's take them up one at a time.

1. Somebody

This, of course, implies a character who engages our interest, makes us care about him or her, and leads us through the journey of the play. Maybe it's a little girl, or a beleaguered king, or a sad young man. Dramaturgically speaking, this person becomes the play's *central character*, or *protagonist*. You will often hear that we have to like, or at least understand, this person well enough to care about the character's destiny. In our situation, it seems to be Red Riding Hood.

2. Wants Something

This implies a specific goal the character wants to achieve, whether it's to get back home, solve the mystery, or find freedom. This element becomes the character's *primary goal*. (Often when a play isn't "going anywhere," the problem lies here.) In our situation, it seems clear that Red wants to get a handful of roses. But is there more to it? Why does she want them? Is there something else going on? Why roses and not morning glories? Why today and not next week? What's really going on; what does she *really* want? We'll come back to this question a bit later.

3. Hard to Get

Drama, as you've often been taught, involves conflict or struggle. If it were easy for Dorothy to get back to Kansas, there would be no *Wizard of Oz* movie. If the chorus told Oedipus who he was right off the bat, we'd have no *Oedipus Rex* play. If Tom could just pick up and leave his sister destitute, we wouldn't be interested in *The Glass Menagerie*. This element—and often there's more than one—becomes a *major obstacle*. (Often when a play isn't interesting or compelling, the problem lies here.) What makes it hard for Red to get those roses? Is she paraplegic? Is she afraid of thorns? Is it raining?

4. And Does Whatever Is Necessary

If a character wants something bad enough, that character will go through whatever it takes to win. He may have to try several different things before any of them works. Dorothy has to find friends, get to the Wizard, kill the witch, and figure out the riddle of the shoes. Oedipus has to threaten, debate, send for people, and probe. Tom has to get a gentleman caller to fall in love with Laura and ensure her future so he can split. These plans are described as *strategies*. (Often when a play is predictable, thin, or dull, the problem lies here.) How is Red going to get those roses if she's afraid of them? How will she get around the fact that it's raining—in fact, the worst storm in twenty-five years? How will she get outside in her wheelchair if there's no ramp?

Thus, a situation becomes dramatic when it contains:

1. A *central character*: Who?
2. A primary *goal* (discussed in chapter 3): Wants *what*?
3. A series of *obstacles* (discussed in chapter 4): *Why* is it difficult?
4. A chain of *strategies* (discussed in chapter 5): *How* to get it?

These are the four elements that comprise the heart of every well-made play. The rest of the chapters of part 1 will look at each of them in turn. Let's begin right now with the first.

Who: The Agent of Action

Sometimes people will tell you they have trouble latching onto a character in your play. You'll hear a variety of comments, the most frequent being, "I don't know whose play this is." (At the risk of being smarmy, I often answer that question by saying, "It's my play; I wrote it.") But what they are really wondering is which character they are supposed to be most invested in: Whom should they care about? Whose adventures should they follow?

Be very careful here. Notice that these two questions involve very different concepts. *Who we are invested in* and *whose adventures we follow* are not always the same thing. For example, take this nursery rhyme:

> Humpty Dumpty sat on a wall;
> Humpty Dumpty had a great fall;
> All the King's horses and all the King's men
> Couldn't put Humpty together again.

Who is the central character, or protagonist, of this little minidrama? At first glance, it seems obvious that it's Humpty. After all, he's the object of our interest; it seems to be about him. He certainly goes through a big change; and without him, nothing would have ever happened. Indeed, it's called "Humpty Dumpty," isn't it?

Sorry. Wrong.

In a sense, all the above reasons are true. But notice now passive Humpty is. He *doesn't do* anything; rather, things *are done* to him. The only thing he even remotely "does" is fall off the wall, and that's only an accident. There's no conscious effort on his part; there's no goal he's in pursuit of; he doesn't undertake any activities in order to accomplish anything. No, the real protagonist of this fable must be somebody else who meets all those requirements. And that, of course, would be the king's men, or perhaps *one* of the king's men. Perhaps Sir Harry. *He* has a problem. *He* has to do something. He has to make things happen. Another way of putting it is that he has to "drive the action forward."

So, while the fable is about Humpty (which puts him at the center), he is not technically the protagonist. In fact, *protagonist* is not the best word to use, since it is so misleading. A better term, which we'll use throughout the rest of this book, is *agent of action,* the person who propels the play forward by actively making things happen.

Could Humpty be made the agent of action in this fable? Possibly, if you changed the word "fell" to "jumped." The difference is moving from the passive to the active.

It's easy, of course, to see how this works in a four-line nursery rhyme. However, look at *Othello*; what do you notice? At first, it seems that Othello is the central character in this play. Indeed, he is: Important things happen to him. He suffers an incredible change in his life; he comes to horrible insights about himself; and he takes control at the end by killing himself. But, *he does not make anything happen*. As I said before, *things happen to him*. Who is it, on the other hand, who really drives the play—convincing other people to act, changing minds, arranging events, and plotting, and scheming, and ultimately winning? Correct: It's Iago. He is the true agent of action. But, you may argue, Othello is so much more important. Clearly Shakespeare meant him to be at the core. You're right. Othello is at the core; however, he's at the core of the *story*, while Iago is at the core of the *play* that tells the story. Remember our discussion of the difference between story and play?

You'll note the same thing is true of *The Glass Menagerie*. The story is about what happens to Laura, but who drives the play forward by making something happen? Tom? No. Amanda.

Are there other plays like this, in which the agent of action is not the central character? Who drives the action in *Macbeth*? Macbeth or his wife and/or the witches? Who drives the action in *A Streetcar Named Desire*? Blanche or Stanley? Who drives the action in *Death of a Salesman*? Willie, Biff, Linda? Who drives the action in *Trifles?*

Exercise 2:1

For each nursery rhyme below, describe who is the agent of action and why. If there is no clearly defined agent, choose one and rewrite the narrative to reveal that.

> Little Miss Muffet sat on her tuffet,
> Eating her curds and whey;
> Along came a spider and sat down beside her
> And frightened Miss Muffet away.

> Old King Cole was a merry old soul,
> And a merry old soul was he;
> He called for his pipe and he called for his bowl
> And he called for his fiddlers three.

> Goosey Goosey Gander,
> Where do you wander?
> Upstairs and Downstairs
> In my lady's chamber.

Revision Questions

In the future, you may hear reactions to your play such as these:

> I couldn't get involved with anybody.
> I didn't know whose play it was.
> It seemed there were two or three plays going on at the same time.
> The main character seemed pretty flimsy and dull.

To help solve these problems, ask yourself the following questions:

1. Have you confused the agent of action with the central character? That is, have you drawn the proper distinction between a character whose fortunes we are interested in and a character *who makes things happen?* In other words, have you written Humpty Dumpty?

2. Which character does the audience seem to gravitate toward? Whom are they most attracted to? Is this the character you want them to be invested in?

3. If your "central character" and the audience's most interesting character are different, what does this tell you? Have you really written another play? Or have you not written this play well enough? Had Shakespeare wanted Othello to be more active, what might he have done differently? Would the play be better or worse for these changes?

4. Is the central character active enough to *be* considered the agent of action? Is the character taking steps or only allowing others to do so?

5. How could you clarify and focus this element? If you don't know how just yet, don't worry: that's what the rest of this book is about.

3

Goals

Our event is becoming slightly more dramatic now. We agree that Red is our agent of action. Now let's examine *what* she wants.

What Do We Mean by Goals?

Actors learn this almost from the first day of beginner's class: in every play—indeed, in every scene—the characters they portray *want something*. They are reaching for a goal. Sometimes that goal is very small and contained within the moment: *I want to get you to give me that apple*. Sometimes that goal is very large and runs through the whole play: *I want to get back to Kansas where I belong*. Playwrights use the same tool. But what do we mean by *goals*, and how do you make them effective? Before we go into that, however, we need to draw a very important and sharp distinction between types of goals. Simply put: Some goals are "inner" and some are "outer." Let me explain.

All of us have deep and basic psychological needs; we all strive to satisfy physical and emotional urges. We want to be safe. We want to be loved. We want to be happy. We want to become successful. We want to express ourselves and be understood. (Gosh, that sounds like playwrights, doesn't it?) These are our inner goals, the drives that compel us forward.

However, all of us differ in the ways in which we translate those inner goals to our external behaviors. I like to ask of each inner goal the basic question, How will you know when you've achieved it? If you want to be happy, how will you know when you are? If you want to be successful, what exactly does that mean? To put it another way:

> What external event or condition has to occur in order for you to say that now, yes, you *are* happy? In other words, how do you translate an unseen "inner" goal into a physical event that we can see or hear?

Another way to consider this is to think of the "inner" goal as a character's motivation, needs, urges; *why* a character does something. Then think of the "outer" goal as the machinery of the story or play, *what* a character does. And remember, it ultimately needs to be seen and/or heard as a physical act.

How Do You Make Outer Goals Work?

To repeat, while all of us share the same "inner" goals, the way in which we translate those into "outer" goals varies. While we all want to achieve success, for Susan, it might be winning an Academy Award. For Gerry, it might be marrying the right spouse. For Ben, it might be earning a million dollars before the age of fifty. For those of you reading this book, it might be writing a hit play. This is in the right direction, but still not home, however. Remember, we are trying to identify *that one event that clearly and physically reveals the inner motive.* Thus, we need to be even more specific.

> *How will you know* when you've won an Academy Award? What external event has to happen? When your name is announced, and you are given a little statue?
>
> *How will you know* when you've married the right spouse? Maybe it's when the preacher pronounces you man and wife? Or maybe it's when you've celebrated your tenth wedding anniversary? Or maybe it's when you have a child?
>
> *How will you know* when you've written a successful play? (What do you mean by "success" anyhow?) Maybe when you open on Broadway? Maybe when the *New York Times* calls you brilliant? Maybe when you've won a Tony? Or maybe when you get your newly found spouse to smile and say, "I'm proud of you"?

Do you see what's happening here? Once you translate the inner goal to an outer goal, you have begun to turn an invisible emotional need into a visible physical action. You are no longer writing a play about "becoming successful"; you are writing a play about "Getting a Tony Award." You are no longer writing a play about "being happy"; you are writing a play about "Finding a way to celebrate a tenth anniversary." Your vague concept has become an outline for a play, containing a physical act that the audience can see, hear, and respond to. (Recall a point I made earlier—that every "change" your character goes through needs somehow to be conveyed by a physical act? Here is the same idea again.)

There's something else equally important happening here. You have begun to illustrate that vague idea of *characterization*. As we've noted, while we all have the same inner drives, the way we choose to satisfy them—the kind of outer goals we set up for ourselves—demonstrates the kind of person we are. Notice that in each of the three examples above, all want something similar, but the different ways they externalize their goals helps you know what kind of people they are.

Assume that your agent of action wants "to become very famous." Different people will translate that need into a different form of How Will He Know? (HWHK, or as in Red's case, HWSK—How Will She Know?). In the following cases, what kind of person does each goal, each HWHK or HWSK, suggest?

Seeing her photo on the front page
Receiving a plaque that reads *Best Citizen*
Being invited to appear on a national news TV show
Being elected class president
Being spoofed on *Saturday Night Live*

Or work the questions from the opposite end: For each of the following kinds of people, what would their "outer" goal become, if their "inner" goal is "to be happy"? Or, again, how would they translate the inner need to an HWHK or HWSK? Be sure to make it a physical act that can be seen or heard.

An egocentric politician _____

A depressed actor _____

A confident athlete _____

A frightened child _____

A lecherous widow _____

What Makes a Goal Dramatic?

So far, so good. You've translated a person's inner need to an external, physical goal. Knowing the external goal, we already have a lot to work with. But there are several additional things to say about goals that will be important and useful. What follows is a list of characteristics that will make your choice of goals, and your plays, more effective. As you conceive your agent's outer goal, consider the following parameters.

1. The Goal Must Be Specific and Visible

We've examined how this works just above. An event must occur that we can see, hear, and understand. Remember, HWHK.

2. The Goal Must Be Completable: It Must Have Some Point at Which It Stops

On the surface, this seems pretty obvious, but writers often find themselves in trouble here because they don't know where the play is heading. When you begin a journey, you usually have a destination in mind, and you know when you will be able to say you have arrived; if you're going to the store, you know you can stop "going" when you've reached the store. Otherwise, you would just keep going and going, and while this may work for the battery bunny, it will soon bore and weary an audience, which will begin thinking, "I don't know where this is headed!"

Think in terms of verbs again. A proper goal should be expressed with a transitive verb or predicate phrase; that is, a verb that takes a direct object, rather than an intransitive (or "state of being") verb, which has no direct object. A good illustration of this principle is *Macbeth*. When asked what his goal is, most people will say, "To be king." However, notice that *be* is an intransitive verb; it goes nowhere and has no end. Better to respond that his goal is "To *become* king," because now we know when, and perhaps how, the action will end: When he has a crown placed upon his head.

The following verbs are intransitive, expressing states of being. Note how they can be changed into predicate phrases with transitive verbs (which also answer HWHK):

To *grow up* could become: To sign the form that opens your own checking account.

To *be in love* could become: To give somebody a wedding ring.

To *be brave* could become: To find the courage to actually cross the threshold of the door that leads into the witch's castle.

To *be happy* could become: To wash your clothes and go see a movie.

And notice how, once you've defined where the goal can end, how much of your play becomes clearer in your head. Go ahead and reread the four goals above. How many images, possible scenes or conflicts, lines of actual dialogue, or possible curtain moments are already bubbling up in the back of your head?

Exercise 3:1

Change the following intransitive verbs to complete predicate phrases with a direction and an end (making sure it's a physical act that can be seen or heard):

To *study harder* could become _____

To *work* could become _____

To *be happy* could become _____

To *be rich* could become _____

To *be more attractive* could become _____

3. The Goal Must Be Positive rather than Negative

To put this another way, your character must want to move toward something rather than away from it. This builds upon the need for the goal to be completable. If you're moving away, you can move and move forever; if you're moving toward, you know where you're going and when you can stop. Thus, for example:

Billy doesn't go out of the room; Billy goes into the kitchen. (The kitchen might be right in the next room, or it might be down the stairs and through the hallway, and he might have to pass the dragon to get there.) Why does Billy go into the kitchen and not the garage?

Sally doesn't leave her marriage; Sally obtains a divorce. (She might have to find the courage, the money, and the lawyer.) Why does Sally get a divorce rather than commit murder?

John doesn't quit smoking; John goes for five days without a cigarette. (These might be the hardest and longest five days of his life!) Why does John take this route and not use hypnotherapy instead?

Exercise 3:2

How would you change each of these negatives into a positive?

Running away from a bad spouse _____

Quitting your old job _____

Moving out of the house _____

4. The Goal Must Be Important, Urgent, Necessary

Playwrights often use the term *at stake* to express this idea: either wondering, "What's at stake for Jim in this play?" or suggesting, "Maybe you could raise the stakes for him more." The more important the goal becomes, the more urgent the need, the greater the drama. It's not enough that Dorothy wants to get back home; what keeps the stakes high is that the witch wants to kill her. It's not enough that Amanda wants to get Laura married; what keeps the stakes high is that, if she doesn't, Laura will be reduced to a penniless, unwanted old maid. It's not enough that Oedipus solves the mystery; what keeps the stakes high is that the city itself is dying.

How urgent is "urgent"? This, of course, is a highly relative matter. What's important to you may not be important to me. However, if I know that this thing *is* important to you, and I care about you, I'll go along for the ride. The challenge, therefore, is to set up the situation so that the stakes are high enough for your character. How can you raise the stakes for Red on her journey to Grandma's house? Well, for one thing, there's a wolf out to eat her; but can you think of something else?

> *Why does Billy need to get to the kitchen?* Is that where the antidote
> for the poison is? Or is he just hungry?
> *Why does Sally need to get divorced?* Is her husband abusive? Or is it
> just because Charlie's richer?
> *Why does John need to quit smoking?* Is he dying of lung cancer? Or
> is it just because he wants to win a bet?

5. Whenever Possible, the Goal Should Somehow Involve Another Person

This other person can be either somebody who can make the goal happen, who stands in the way of the goal, or who might be needed to help. Dorothy can't get home alone. Amanda can't get a date for Laura without Tom. Oedipus needs to find answers from the people who know. Iago can't destroy Othello without there first being an Othello.

Take a look at some of the other goals we've come up with. What happens to the situation when you add another person into it?

> Billy doesn't go out of the room; Billy goes into the kitchen—*but
> he has to defy Steve in order to do so.*
> Sally doesn't leave her marriage; Sally obtains a divorce—*but she
> needs to hire a lawyer first.*
> John doesn't quit smoking; John goes for five days without a ciga-
> rette—*all the time living with a roommate who smokes like a chimney.*

Skipping ahead to the subject of the next chapter, consider the following *obstacles*:

> What happens when Steve refuses to let Billy pass?
> What happens when the lawyer Sally wants to hire refuses to take
> her case?
> What happens when John's roommate has made a bet with a third
> person that he can make John fail?

It's useful again to look at the work of actors here. One way of looking at a play is to see it as a series of negotiations. Each moment, whether large or small, is at bottom really about somebody in some situation with another person in which that somebody is trying to get something from the other person. Thus, the goal is really about convincing somebody to do something. This seems a small point, but it's an essential one: The goal is not getting John to open the door for me; the goal is about convincing John that he should turn the handle. (You will know you've reached it when you see John perform that physical act.) The goal is not getting engaged to Susan; the goal is about convincing Susan to utter the word: "Yes." (You'll know you've reached it when you hear the sound come out of her mouth.) The goal is not about encouraging Billy to stand up for himself; the goal is about convincing Billy he should say, "This is my toy!" (Again, you'll know you've reached it when you hear that sound come from his mouth.) Note that in each of these examples, we are being very specific as regards (1) what's really going on in the scene, and (2) what is the exact physical act the character is striving to accomplish.

Actors are taught to examine each line they speak in order to discover why they are saying that line; that is, what goal they are trying to reach. It's the writer's job to make sure of the same thing.

Exercise 3:3

Revise these goals to make them more specific, considering them as attempts to convince another person to perform some physical act, as in the first example:

> I want Joan to agree with me. (*I want to convince Joan to say, "Yes, you're right."*)
> I want John to give me the keys. (*I want to convince John to . . . ?*)
> I want Steve to buy me another drink.
> I want Gertrude to confess. (About what?)
> I want Laura to tell me why she's missing school.
> I want my teacher to give me an "A" for this class.

How Revising Goals Can Improve Your Play

We've spent a lot of time on this one element, noting several important concepts:

- Goals are both "inner" and "outer."
- But the outer goal is the one the audience responds to and the one you write.
- Outer goals help define your characters—what they choose to pursue tells us a lot about them.
- Goals can be large—taking a whole play to accomplish.
- Or goals can be small—each individual moment in a play is a negotiation of sorts that has its own immediate goal.
- Goals that are dramatically effective have the five characteristics described above (see the section titled, What Makes a Goal Dramatic?).

I hope you've noticed what's happened here. As we've gone through each individual characteristic of goals, the story of the play has become clearer and more focused. We've gradually come to understand where the play is headed; we've begun to see what other characters we need and how they can be used; we've made the situation compelling and urgent; we've even begun to suggest dialogue for the scene.

You will often find that when your play gets bogged down, confused, or static, most of the time the problem is an unfocused, inactive, negative, or weak goal.

A Challenge

Before we leave this discussion of goals, I'd like to present you with a challenge. I've used material from *Macbeth* to illustrate important points along the way; let's use it once more. Do you recall a few pages ago we said that Macbeth's major outer goal is to become king? Perhaps you have already noted one slight problem: Macbeth achieves this goal at the end of act 2. He's killed Duncan and got himself crowned. His goal has been met. But there are still three more acts of the play left! *Now what is he after?* What occupies him for the last three acts? In other words, what is he really after, of which *becoming king* is just one small first step?

As you search for an answer, please apply the five criteria mentioned above. Perhaps one of these suggestions will work for you: Macbeth wants to:

- become the most powerful man in Scotland, by first becoming king and then securing his power by killing all potential rivals.
- demonstrate to the "witches," or whatever they represent, that he is master of his own fate and can control events around him.
- show his wife that he's a strong guy after all.

Or perhaps there is something else you can see more clearly than I do.

Exercise 3:4

Here is a situation for a play: Steve and John are sitting in a bar. Steve has just announced to John that he's getting married to Betty. John doesn't think Steve is making a good decision and tries to tell him so.

What's wrong with this situation as it's described? Several things. Let's note them and fix them. As we do, keep in mind your play and consider how these same steps might help you clarify what's fuzzy or invent what's missing:

It's vague and unfocused. We don't know who our *agent of action* is. Let's say it's John.

It has no direction. John has no specific goal. "Trying to tell Steve" is somewhere in the ballpark, but still a little too vague. Let's give him something more specific: let's say he wants to stop the marriage.

But how will he know (HWHK)? How will he know when he has stopped the marriage? When he convinces Steve to do something very specific and observable. But what should that be? What exactly does he want from Steve? In other words, how can the five characteristics of goals be helpful here?

1. Something specific and physical.
2. Something completable.
3. Something positive.
4. Something urgent.
5. Something involving another person.

Let's say John wants Steve to promise him that he'll break it off with Betty. John wants Steve to make that promise tonight, since the ceremony is tomorrow. John wants Steve to shake hands on the deal, since shaking hands was always their childhood solemn pact-binder. In other words, this scene is now about John convincing Steve to shake hands about cancelling the wedding.

Hopefully, something interesting happened in your head when you read that. Perhaps the situation suddenly became more interesting to you. Perhaps you saw it more clearly. Perhaps even lines of dialogue bubbled into your head. In many ways, once you clarify this goal, half of the scene is already finished!

Now, it's your turn. Here is another situation for a play: Mark and Diane are hitchhiking to get to Chicago. They're in a small town, stranded. They have maxed out their credit cards and only have a couple dollars between them. They are sitting in a park. Create and write a five-minute play. Select who your agent will be and define a specific goal. Once you've done that, the rest is typing.

Revision Questions

When people critique your play, they may make comments such as these:

> It didn't seem to have a direction.
> I couldn't understand where it was going.
> I couldn't follow the character; she didn't make sense; I didn't know what she was after.
> The ending didn't seem to fit.
> I really didn't care about the situation; the stakes didn't seem high enough.

All these comments indicate that a clear and driving line of action is missing so far.

Ask yourself these questions:

1. Do you understand your character's "inner" goal? Do you know yet what emotional need is driving him or her to action?

2. Have you embodied that "inner" goal into the right "outer"? Have you translated the character goal to the best story goal?

3. Have you been able to specifically identify the HWHK factor? In other words, is your character's outer goal specific, objective, and identifiable enough? What one physical act is needed?

4. Is the goal positive or negative? Have you confused the two? Can you specify what your agent of action is going for? Is this specific and observable enough?

5. Are the stakes high enough? What possible ways can you make achieving this goal of utmost urgency? If it were a life-and-death matter, what would be involved?

6. Does this goal require the help of other characters? Whom must your agent of action interact with? How are those relationships crucial? How can they be clarified or strengthened?

7. Now review all of your characters in the play. It's often said that every character is the agent of action of his or her own version of the story, and in many ways this is true. Can you, therefore, apply all of the rules about goals to *each character* in the play? Are you specific enough? If you were to make a chart for each character, what would it look like, and what would it teach you about the play?

4

Obstacles

We know that Red is our agent of action. We know that her goal is to pick a dozen roses. Now we need to add the third key: making it difficult for her to do so. Here's where we add that oh-so-important thing called *conflict*.

What Do Obstacles Do?

The first and primary thing that *obstacles* do, of course, is keep your play interesting. However, there is a second and equally important function that obstacles serve, and that is to enrich the play's *characterization*. If you recall, in the last chapter we came to realize that characters can often be defined by the goals they create for themselves. Because Iago wants to destroy Othello—rather than just remain annoyed with him—he is revealed as a certain kind of person, and not a nice one at that. But we also get to know about him through the obstacles Shakespeare creates, each of which is designed to reveal part of Iago's character. Let's look at a few of them.

In the first act, Iago is plagued by Roderigo, a foolish fop who wants Iago to help him seduce Desdemona. He keeps annoying Iago and insisting on his attention. As he is forced to find ways to deal with Roderigo, Iago reveals a clever but sneaky side of his personality. Ultimately, Iago is forced to kill him, revealing an ever darker part of himself.

One of Iago's schemes involves convincing Othello's friend Cassio to get drunk. However, an obstacle emerges: Cassio does not drink. Thus, Iago has to become very soldierly, very convivial and sociable: We get to see him as a man who is well-liked, manly, and able to carry a tune. He becomes a charming good fellow. One could almost like him.

Another obstacle is Desdemona herself: her reputation is unassailable. In fact, she is so well regarded that Iago arrives at a dead-end; there's nothing he can do. But then she drops her handkerchief, and we now see a side of Iago that is quick-witted and intelligent enough that he immediately knows how to make use of it.

Another obstacle appears in Iago's own wife, Emilia; she defends Othello's innocence and starts to berate her husband. And we get to see a side of Iago that is so vicious he'll even commit murder.

Thus, Iago becomes defined for us by how he reacts to, and deals with, the people that stand in his way. Shakespeare has carefully selected those obstacles, perhaps deliberately, in order for parts of Iago's personality to come forward. (In this respect, obstacles are very closely related to *strategies*; a point we'll deal with more extensively in the next chapter.)

Where Do Obstacles Come From?

What follows in this section is a brief list of where obstacles might originate. It is certainly not meant to be comprehensive, but rather a quick guide to stimulate your imagination. After having finished your first draft, you may think you've explored and exhausted all your possibilities. Maybe not. Be open to unusual possibilities. Do any of these apply to your play? Could they? Think outside your preconceived ideas and explore the unusual. There's always the delete key. (I'll be inventing examples from "Little Red Riding Hood" just for the fun of it. You try with "Sleeping Beauty" and see what you come up with.)

Some Obstacles Are Built into the Situation from the Very Beginning

Obstacles may be inherent within the circumstances of the play's world. These need to be introduced early in the play, as foreshadowing, and then brought to the foreground as the play progresses. They include the following:

1. What is the nature of the agent's goal?

How far-reaching and difficult is the goal to begin with? Red has to go to Grandma's house, but it isn't just down the street. It's in the middle of a deep, dark forest. It's winter and gets dark early.

2. What's at stake for the agent? Why is it urgent?

Red has to get there before nightfall, because strange things happen after dark. Grandma is quite ill and needs the sugar that the cookies contain. Red's mom has threatened to punish Red if she fails this mission.

3. Where is the agent most vulnerable?

This is closely allied to what's at stake for her but speaks more to an internal emotional condition rather than an external factor. Red is terrified of the dark. Red has no sense of direction. Red has issues with her Grandma who always puts her down and calls her fat. Red wants to be a movie star.

4. What other people are in this world?

This is one of the reasons why you should try to give your agent a goal that requires in some way the assistance of somebody else. If "somebody else" says, "No!" or perhaps, "Yes, but only if . . .," then you've got something to work with.

> *People who might want to stop her.* Rumors are afloat that the wolf is on the prowl again. Red's mom is evil and wants her death to look like an accident. Grandma herself is cantankerous, deaf, and incontinent.
>
> *People who might want to help her if she can convince them to.* Where there are woods, there are often woodsmen; one might likely be in the woods right now. Who can she trust?

Other Obstacles Might Be Introduced
Later in the Play as They Are Needed

1. An unexpected event occurs, caused by some external force

> A new character unexpectedly shows up.
> The woodsman has a wife who doesn't want him taking his gun to work.

Somebody dies. Red's mom suffers a heart attack just before Red sets out.

Somebody makes an unexpected move, doing something that the agent did not expect. The woodsman suddenly wants sex.

An act of natural force intervenes. The weather, the river, the volcano, or the snake suddenly becomes active.

The worst thing that could happen—whatever it is that Red's most afraid of—indeed does happen, and she has to face her fear. Red meets the wolf in the deep, dark forest.

Things that were expected to happen don't. The road sign isn't there after all.

People who were supposed to help aren't there. The old hermit has gone to visit his daughter.

Time is running out. It's getting near the darkening hour. Grandma's medication is wearing off. Red isn't getting any younger. The bomb's set to go off in seven seconds.

2. An unexpected revelation is made; something that wasn't known before is suddenly discovered

From the past: Red's long-lost cousin shows up and vows to help her get rid of Mom.

From another character: The woodsman is married after all and has just been toying with Red's affections.

About the truth or reality of the situation itself: Another thing the long-lost cousin reveals is that Red is illegitimate and is really the princess of Spain. Red's Grandma is a wolf; the bounty hunter has been a double agent all along.

3. The agent suddenly sees things differently and it changes her goal

Often, this is the result of the unexpected revelation. There's more need for Red to be terrified of Grandma, especially now that she's only pretending to be sick and helpless.

4. An aspect of the agent's personality, which has lain dormant all this time, is suddenly thrust to the surface

Red is more cowardly than she thought. She suddenly has scruples about committing grandmatricide.

Sidebar

We've been looking at obstacles as sources of blockage and difficulty. Things come from many places to hinder. But anything that forms an obstacle can also be a help. At any point in your play, any one of the above items can appear and be helpful. The woodsman that Red meets might be an ally after all. Red might suddenly realize she's *braver* than she thought.. And Grandma may turn out to be a guardian angel in the end!

As you can see, the above list offers many suggestions and many sources for creating obstacles. Let's put theory into practice.

Exercise 4:1

Here's a famous nursery rhyme:

> Old King Cole was a merry old soul,
> And a merry old soul was he;
> He called for his pipe, he called for his bowl,
> And he called for his fiddlers three.

How would you create obstacles for this fellow? Answer the following questions:

1. What does Cole want? What is his outer goal? HWHK? In other words, what exactly does he want from the three fiddlers, and how will he know when he has it?

2. Why is this goal inherently difficult? What is there about the situation, the times, or the nature of the three fiddlers that is going to make it hard from the beginning?

3. What's at stake for Cole? Where is he vulnerable? What circumstance can you create that would bring that vulnerability to the surface?

4. Who are the characters opposing him? Who doesn't want Cole to get those fiddlers or to let them play?

5. What new character can you introduce that makes things a little more complicated?

6. What new character can you create who could help?

7. What force of nature could play a part?

8. As the play progresses, what does Cole learn that makes a difference? About the past? About the fiddlers? About the situation itself? About himself?

Exercise 4:2

Write a five-minute play, using these directions: On the first page, make sure you clearly introduce your *agent of action* and his or her *goal*. Also be sure to establish one element of the situation that makes achieving the goal hard (i.e., choose one from the list of obstacles already built into the situation).

Over the next two pages, let us see what your agent does to overcome those obstacles.

On page 3 or 4, introduce an unexpected event from that section of the list above. Let us see how your character deals with this obstacle.

On page 5 or 6, introduce a new revelation into the picture, from any of the items on that section of the list above. Let us see how your character deals with this obstacle.

By the end of the play, on page 6 or 7, show us whether your character succeeds or not.

Revision Questions

As you work on future drafts, you may often hear responses such as these:

> I thought it was dull in spots.
> I didn't think the stakes were high enough.
> I couldn't understand what the problem was.
> There wasn't enough conflict. (Or) I couldn't understand what the conflict was. (Or) Why couldn't she have simply called the police?

These indicate your work might be lacking sufficient obstacles. Ask yourself the following questions:

1. Do you have sufficient obstacles for your agent of action to deal with?

2. Are they strong enough? Are the stakes high enough?

3. Have you chosen effective obstacles? Do they help reveal your agent of action's personality?

4. Are there others—possibly from the list—that you can invent, which will be more useful and pertinent?

5

Strategies

Red is out picking roses. It started off as a nice sunny day with no obstacles in view. Suddenly, obstacles appear. Her brother starts to fling mud pies at her. Or it starts to rain. Or she can't find her scissors. Or her childhood fear of sharp thorns starts to bother her. Which one or ones should we choose?

Well, we know we want to choose one or more that best reveal her character. For now, let's assume we want Red to be a smart and pleasant person who isn't afraid of anything. So perhaps her bratty brother. Let's choose that for now, since it's always better to involve another character.

Now, the question to consider is: How will Red overcome this obstacle? How will she convince her brother to go back in the house where he belongs? We are now in the category of *strategies*—those schemes and plans your agent of action undertakes to get what she wants.

How many strategies do you need? Where do they come from? How do you best use them? We'll answer these questions one at a time, but first please notice that, just like goals and obstacles, strategies come in many sizes; you might say that the "size" of the strategy pretty much depends on the "size" of the obstacle it is dealing with. Thus, Dorothy sets up a very large strategy in order to get home—she has to befriend the Wizard. However, when she is faced with the Tin Woodman's rustiness, her strategy is relatively quick and immediate: she reaches for the oil can.

(Hopefully, this will be easy, and she won't discover that a charm has been placed on the oil can that lets it be lifted only if you speak the magic words—in which case Dorothy has a whole new obstacle, requiring a whole different set of strategies.).

So, Red picking roses seems a small goal and might just call for a few strategies. We'll see as we go along.

Strategies Reveal Character

Just as selecting the right goal and the right obstacles helps reveal character, so does selecting the right strategies. How characters go about getting what they want is as revealing as knowing what they want and what they have to fight to get it. Dorothy chooses to obey the dictates of Glinda and travel to Emerald City, rather than to organize the Munchkins into a rebellious army of guerillas. She chooses to tame the Lion and make him an ally, rather than to lead the Scarecrow and Tin Man in a fight against him.

In *Othello,* notice that every single strategy Iago chooses to achieve his goal and to overcome the obstacles he meets are dark, immoral, treacherous, and downright bad. Of course, this is intentional, since Shakespeare intends him to be evil personified. But take a look at Amanda, in *The Glass Menagerie.* Her major goal is to make sure that Laura is provided for. Amanda's first strategy, before the play opens, appears to have been to enroll Laura in business school so that she can learn an employable skill. This, of course, fails, since Laura gets sick in class and drops out. So Amanda is now faced with creating new strategies.

What does she do? She tries to find Laura a husband. A romantic, somewhat idealistic and almost silly idea, but very characteristic of Amanda. But now consider what she does not do: Any number of things that a more realistic and practical person might attempt, such as getting Laura counseling, homeschooling her, enrolling her in another program, or teaching Laura how to sell magazines by phone (as Amanda herself does). Of course, if Amanda had chosen any of these, it would be a very different play. And that, of course, is the point.

Now, what about Red and her miserable sibling? She might choose several strategies, each showing us a different person. What if she bribes him with candy? What if she calls and complains to mom? What if she ignores him? What if she seduces him? What if she kills him?

Exercise 5:1

Consider a character who wants to graduate college with highest honors. What sort of strategies might be generated by each of the following personalities?

1. A deceitful, ambitious person
2. An ex-marine who believes in the code of honor
3. A beautiful but very dumb young lady
4. The younger brother of Albert Einstein
5. Brad Pitt

So, the kind of strategies you create are important purveyors of character. Strategies come in large and small sizes. Now, how do you use what you've created?

Strategies Are All Connected

The most important thing to understand about strategies is that they are all connected. When you stop to analyze it, most human behavior is a series of strategies, all connected to each other in complicated webs of relationships. Some, you might say, are self-contained. Most, however, require us to do other things first: this is where the concept of *in order to* becomes important, and we can start to talk about what we'll call *substrategies*.

At other times, we have to reevaluate our plan because we've come across an obstacle that we hadn't considered. We run into what we'll call a *however* and have to come up with something we'll call a *side strategy*. Or we finish one strategy, only to find out that it wasn't right: it didn't work. We have *failed strategies*.

For example, you're hungry. You decide upon an early-morning goal: to have a bowl of cereal with milk for breakfast. On the surface, it seems simple. But consider how many substrategies it takes to make that happen. You have to put the cereal into a bowl. In order to do that, however, you first have to get the cereal out of the cupboard. In order to do that, you have to open the cupboard. Before that, you have to get to the cupboard. You have to go into the kitchen. You have to get out of bed. You have to open your eyes. See how far back in time you have to go?

And that's just to get the cereal. You also need a side strategy. You also have to get the milk; and this has its own series of substrategies. You have to open the new carton of milk you bought last night; you have to find the carton in the back of the crowded top shelf; you have to open the refrigerator; and you have to get to the refrigerator.

Now you have to get a spoon. You have to find a clean one in the drawer. However, you notice there are no clean ones. Side strategy: you have to wash a dirty one from last night. But first—here comes a *however*—you have to find one in the pile of dishes still in the sink. Then, you have to locate, reach, open, and use the dishwashing detergent somewhere in the clutter under the sink, only to find that the bottle you thought was detergent is really the bottle of shower cleaner you were looking for last week.

We could go on and on. It might eventually take you half an hour and a few dozen steps to get through before you can finally put a spoonful of milk and cereal in your mouth. Or you might become frustrated about the spoon-washing, chuck the whole idea (a *failed strategy* at work), and decide to drive over to McDonalds . . . but then, of course, you have to find your car keys, which are in your pants somewhere in your room. It's now 8:30, and you still haven't gotten anywhere near achieving your goal.

And this is just breakfast!

Plays work the same way. The same complicated interweaving of strategies—substrategies, side strategies, and failed strategies—drives the action and becomes, essentially, the content of the work. If you put them all into a list, working backwards, and label each step as either a substrategy, a side strategy, or a failed strategy, you might have something like this for *The Glass Menagerie*.

What is Amanda's goal? To provide security for Laura.

IN ORDER TO PROVIDE SECURITY (HWSK?— How will she know?
Look back at our discussion of goals in chapter 3), Amanda has
to get Laura married.

IN ORDER TO GET HER MARRIED, she has to get somebody to propose to Laura.

IN ORDER TO GET HIM TO PROPOSE, she has to impress him.

Here the tree splits into side strategies, some of which are:

getting fancy clothes,
replacing an old lampshade with a new one,
preparing a special dinner,
finding out what he likes to eat,

and so on. But first, before she can impress him, she has to get a
man *to meet Laura.*

IN ORDER TO DO THAT, she has to get Tom to invite somebody to
come over.

HOWEVER, she's had a quarrel with Tom and first has to make up
with him.

IN ORDER TO DO THAT, . . .

Look at scene 4. Amanda speaks the following lines in which she
is clearly working a minor but very important and connected
strategy: "Tom. I sent out your sister so I could discuss something
with you. If you hadn't spoken, I would have spoken to you." In
other words, she has to send Laura out of the room so she can
speak to Tom, so she can make up with him, so she can convince
him to invite somebody for dinner, so she can impress this man
and get him to like Laura, so he'll eventually propose marriage
and Laura will eventually be provided for . . . and Amanda will
have done her motherly duty. Do you see the principle?

Essentially, every line in your play is really the bottom of a
very long series of strategies designed to get your agent to complete a goal. Each moment is there *in order to* help the agent move
forward. So, if you work backwards from the key climactic moment and note the steps it takes to get there, the substrategies,
side strategies, and failed strategies you've had to weave through,

you'll wind up with a fairly complete, cohesive, and comprehensive outline of your entire play. An excellent book by David Ball, *Backwards and Forwards: A Technical Manual for Reading Plays* (Southern Illinois University Press, 1983), is all about this process. It is highly recommended.

And also notice what you have at the bottom of these lengthy, interwoven in-order-to lists: a line of dialogue. Or, as we discussed in chapter 1, a physical action that the audience can see and/or hear.

To restate: Every single moment in the play is a physical act that is part of a strategy that some character performs in order to complete his or her goal. And, by generating an in-order-to chart that works backwards from the climax of your play—when your agent achieves his or her goal—you can do several things:

1. Fill your play with interesting actions that reveal character.
2. Build slowly from one moment to the next.
3. Make sure that your play is focused.

For an extended example, get out your copy of *Othello* and locate the brief scene between Iago and Cassio in act 2, scene 3. By now, we know that Iago is out to destroy Othello. In this scene, Iago is becoming very chummy with Cassio and sings with him a little drinking song:

IAGO:
> Some wine, ho!
> (*Sings*)
> And let me the canakin clink, clink;
> And let me the canakin clink
> A soldier's a man;
> A life's but a span;
> Why, then, let a soldier drink.
> Some wine, boys!

Why is he performing this physical act of singing and drinking? Working backwards, fill in the blanks for an in-order-to chart that begins as follows:

> *To get Othello to destroy himself,* Iago must _____
>
> IN ORDER TO DO THAT, he must _____
> IN ORDER TO DO THAT, he must _____
> IN ORDER TO DO THAT, he must _____
> IN ORDER TO DO THAT, he must _____
> IN ORDER TO DO THAT, he must _____
> IN ORDER TO DO THAT, he must _____
> IN ORDER TO DO THAT, he must _____

Your answers might look like this:

> get Othello to kill himself in shame,
> get Othello to kill Desdemona,
> convince Othello that Desdemona is cheating on him with Cassio,
> get Desdemona to intercede on Cassio's behalf after Cassio's been fired,
> get Cassio fired,
> get Cassio to cause a disturbance in the town,
> get Cassio drunk enough to do that,
> get Cassio to take one cup of wine.

All those strategies, carefully connected and interwoven, work directly or indirectly toward the satisfaction of Iago's ultimate goal. Indeed, a few lines earlier in the same scene, Iago has himself articulated this very chain:

> If I can fasten but one cup upon him,
> With that which he hath drunk to-night already,
> He'll be as full of quarrel and offence
> As my young mistress' dog. Now, my sick fool Roderigo,
> Whom love hath turn'd almost the wrong side out,
> To Desdemona hath to-night caroused
> Potations pottle-deep; and he's to watch:
> Three lads of Cyprus, noble swelling spirits,
> That hold their honours in a wary distance,
> The very elements of this warlike isle,
> Have I to-night fluster'd with flowing cups,
> And they watch too. Now, 'mongst this flock of drunkards,

Am I to put our Cassio in some action
That may offend the isle.

$$(2.3.45-57)$$

Exercise 5:2

Consider this situation: You're a shy young man who wants to get Judy to say that she will marry you. (Notice the goal I've laid out for you requires Judy to actually "say" she will marry you; remember that goals have to involve physical activities.)

Fill in the chart below with whatever strategies fit:

IN ORDER TO get Judy to say yes, you must _____

IN ORDER TO DO THAT, you must _____

IN ORDER TO DO THAT, you must _____

IN ORDER TO DO THAT, you must _____

HOWEVER, an *obstacle* appears. (What is it?) _____

IN ORDER TO get around that obstacle (side strategy), you must ___

_____

Now, making sure that the answer to this next one is a physical act, finish the chart:

IN ORDER TO DO THAT, you must say the following words, or perform the
following activity: _____

Now look at what you've done: you have actually written a line of dialogue or stage business.

Extraordinary Strategies

One final point to make about strategies before we move on: Strategies ought to be surprising; insofar as possible, try to create unusual options for your character, showing new sides of this person and at the same time giving the audience a jolt of novelty.

Consider Iago again, and return to the scene in act 2, when Iago's goal is to convince Cassio to take one drink. Shakespeare has Iago sing—a good choice; it reveals character, gets the job done, and perhaps even pleases the audience a little. But at the same time, a little predictable for a soldier, isn't it? Perhaps too easy? What else might Iago have done? Here's a list I've typed completely at random:

> Challenged him to a round of poker or its Elizabethan equivalent;
> Bet him on the best two out of three dart games;
> Blackmailed him with the information that Iago knew Cassio was gay;
> Shamed Cassio by calling him a sissy weakling;
> Gotten a woman in the bar to seduce Cassio into taking a drink;
> Gotten Roderigo to secretly sneak some alcohol into Cassio's glass of water.

Take a moment yourself right now and create a half-dozen more. If you're having trouble thinking of realistic ones, invent fantastic ones. Perhaps Iago knows magic or hypnotism. Create as long a list as you can. And then look at it carefully, to see if there's something more unusual, revelatory of character, and surprising that your character can choose.

Now look again at Amanda. We discussed above how characteristic of Amanda it is that she chooses as a strategy to ensure Laura's survival finding a way to get her married. In that section, we considered other options she might have chosen. Just for practice, take a moment and jot down ten more options different from those. How else might Amanda have protected Laura? Again, make bold and unusual choices. Could any of them have made an interesting play?

Exercise 5:3

Choose any short scene you've written for this book or from the first draft of the play you're working on. Write at the top of a sheet your agent of action and the agent's goal (e.g., Mary wants to convince her mother to agree that she can become a nun.). Now write ten strategies Mary might try. Then write ten more. Then write ten more. None of these strategies has to be realistic; in fact, the more outrageous the better. The idea is to loosen up your mind and search for strategies out of the ordinary. What did you discover? Did Mary surprise you in any way? If so, use what you've found and surprise your audience as well.

REVISION QUESTIONS

As you develop your play, you may encounter reactions such as these:

> It bogged down in spots.
>
> I got lost in the middle; the play seemed to veer off into a completely different direction from where it was headed. I couldn't follow it.
>
> It was too predictable; I knew what was coming.
>
> It didn't make sense. Why did the character jump out the window when he could have used the door?
>
> It all seemed like the same kind of action.
>
> The character didn't seem consistent. I don't think a man like that would do such a thing.
>
> It seemed like a lot of psychobabble; I got bored hearing people complain.

Here are a few questions to ask yourself:

1. What is the climactic moment of your play?

2. Can you create an in-order-to chart that flows logically from this point back to the beginning of your play?

3. Are there gaps in logic? Have you assumed certain things are related when in fact they are not?

4. Have you determined how side strategies impact your agent's quest? Have you created enough? Too many?

5. Have you exhausted all possible strategies? If you were to force yourself to jot down thirty different possibilities for any one of your chart's steps, would you find anything more interesting, characteristic, and surprising that might be useful?

Part Two

Putting Them Together

6

Plot

We've examined the basic elements that underlie every traditional well-made play, these being the four keys, and noted that they are the basic building blocks of your play's structure. Now let's consider how best to use them. We'll answer such questions as: How do you put all of these components into a whole play? How do you give them shape and coherence? How do you know what comes first, how to start, where and how to indicate where the play is going, and other matters?

Which, of course, brings us to the large question of *plot*—putting it all together. But first, a brief aside. Any discussion of plot, especially in the kinds of plays we're talking about, always and by necessity brings us to Aristotle and his *Poetics*. Aristotle was a Greek philosopher whose manic curiosity led him to analyze nearly every aspect of the natural and metaphysical world in order to find out exactly what things were and how they worked. He loved to classify and define things, both physical and theoretical. At one point, he put his mind to the plays he saw being written and performed around him, by such writers as Sophocles, Aeschylus, and Euripides. Not bad for role models.

His musings on drama have come down to us in his work *Poetics* in which he scrutinized as many tragedies as he could and distilled his findings. What he wrote was not so much a book on how to write a play as a survey on the things that all the great plays he studied had in common. Which, if you look at it, is really "How to write a play," coming in the back door. The first part of this chapter, therefore, is a brief summary of what he found.

Defining a Play

Aristotle began by defining what a play is. (Earlier in this book, I did too, and some of my definition is borrowed from his.) For him, a play is

> an imitation of an action that is serious, complete, and of significant magnitude; in language embellished with each kind of artistic ornament, the several kinds being found in separate parts of the play; in the form of action, not of narrative; through pity and fear effecting the proper purgation of these emotions. (*Poetics* 6.1449b.24–29)

Let's take this sentence in small doses and translate them into concepts that you can use. (Some of them you've already met in this book.)

An Imitation . . .

He seems to be saying that what the playwright presents on the stage is a reflection of actual life. This does not mean it's a picture of an event as it happened, but rather a picture of the writer's interpretation of it. You can't show actual life on the stage: it's too happenstance—things often occur without any meaning; and it's too dull. Most of us spend our days going through a regimen of existence that would be painfully boring to watch. In short, an actual picture would be too random or too confusing or too simple to have any meaning for us. No, the writer's job is not to show life, but to reflect and comment on it. I'll have more to say about this further on.

Of an Action . . .

We've discussed the term *action* before. Refer to chapter 1 and note the component parts of action. And notice how it must have a certain structural shape to it. It's not random; it has to involve what? Yes, a change.

That Is Serious, Complete, . . .

The term *complete* here means that it has a wholeness about it, a sense that a "oneness" has occurred, whatever that "oneness" is. Later on, Aristotle will define *complete* as that which has a beginning, a middle, and an end. But what is *it* that comes to an end? What constitutes *this* "wholeness," *this* "oneness?" Refer to chapter 1 and our discussion of what we mean by "an event." The term *serious* seems appropriate because Aristotle is talking about tragedy. But he means something more here than just "mood"; he means that there is a sense of significance about the event; something that has resonance or meaning; something, if you will, that you "can take away with you." Sometimes you've heard this idea expressed as *theme*.

And of Significant Magnitude; . . .

By this, Aristotle means size or length, if you will. He notes that great plays are the right size. "But," you well may ask, "what does that mean? How long should a play be?" Aristotle provides an answer—but not in chronological time. For him, it makes no difference if the play is one minute or nine hours long (and there are plays that are examples of each). For him, the clock is internal. In a later section of *Poetics,* he defines what that internal clock is. He says, "The play should be of sufficient size to effect a Change of Fortune" in somebody's life. Again, we've met this concept before, in chapter 1. A play has to be long enough for this major change to take place—and you'll recall how many different kinds of changes are possible.

In Language Embellished with Each Kind of Artistic Ornament, the Several Kinds Being Found in Separate Parts of the Play; . . .

I'm going to cheat a bit here. If you have had any theater history, you know something about the Greek theater and drama that Aristotle was familiar with. The plays were largely poetic dramas. They involved characters struggling with fate and destiny. They were often structured as scenes between two characters, interspersed with choral odes, long passages sung and danced by a group of people who were ancillary to the action. For Aristotle, each of these individual moments called for a different kind of dialogue: some simple, some complex, some direct, some allusive, and so on. These conventions no longer apply to the kinds of play we're talking about, and so we'll pass over this section and move on to . . .

In the Form of Action, Not Narrative; . . .

By this, he means that we are watching actors perform events for us on the stage as though they were really happening, as opposed to hearing a storyteller simply tell us the events. I could sit you down and tell you all about what happened to Dorothy in Oz, but it's better for you to "watch" these events unfold. Why? Because it's more involving, more exciting, more meaningful, and a heck of a lot more fun. We'll explore this concept further in the chapter on *miniplays*.

Through Pity and Fear Effecting a Proper Purgation of These Emotions

We're in a little bit of trouble here, for scholars over the centuries have not quite agreed on what this means. What are "pity and fear"? What does he mean by "purgation"? (Other translations use the word "catharsis"). We don't have time for, nor interest in, this argument. For now, let it suffice just to generalize and say that, for Aristotle, the best plays somehow draw an emotional response out of us. We become involved in people very much like us, who have experiences that could happen to us, and we somehow are affected by this. And being affected is a good thing; it makes us, somehow, better people.

In other words, a great deal of what's in this book is a reflection on what Aristotle discovered over three thousand years ago. The fact that successful, well-made plays still follow these precepts is an indication of how important they are.

Aristotle's Key Ingredients

As Aristotle examined the successful plays of his time, he found that they all contained within them six different components: call them "ingredients" or "parts." They are as follows:

1. PLOT: The sequence of events that we watch unfold; the series of happenings that make up the overall dramatic action. Earlier I explained that this dramatic action itself contained four key elements, which I called the building blocks of the play: Agent of Action, Goal, Obstacle, and Strategy. Consider all four of these collectively making up that component which Aristotle calls "plot."

2. CHARACTER: The people who take part in these events.

3. THOUGHT: The ideas that these people express (often translated as *theme*).

4. LANGUAGE: The forms of verse, the use of words, the shaping of ideas into verbal communication (often translated as *dialogue*).

5. MUSIC: The forms of singing and dancing typical of the kind of plays Aristotle watched (often translated as *sound*, which is inaccurate).

6. SPECTACLE: The visual impressions we receive; that is, scenery, costumes, lighting, and so forth. What is included in "so forth" doesn't concern us here.

Of these six, we're going to spend the rest of this chapter on the first.

What Is Plot?

Aristotle puts the first component, *plot*, above every other, calling it the most important aspect of the play. It is not the language nor the personalities that affect us most; it's the sequence of events that take place. Indeed, he says that in the best plays, the spectator only has to learn of the story—the sequence of events—to be moved already.

You know this is true because you read TV listings or movie blurbs. You read that this film is "about a man who murders his father and has sex with his mother," and you decide whether or not to go see that. Or you hear your friend say, "The movie was all about this woman in the nineteenth century who wanted to be a doctor and had to fight the whole male establishment to get a chance," and you are either affected enough to go see it or bored enough to turn on the cable poker channel instead.

How does Aristotle define plot? (And you know he does!) In very simple terms that have important resonance: "the selection and arrangement of the incidents." Let's turn to them now.

Selection

Selection means that you are very careful in deciding what to put in your play: what events over the course of the action you choose to show on stage. Recall that in chapter 1 we noted the difference between the totality of Red Riding Hood's life and just that part of it which we decided to use in our play. We chose just that part that had meaning for us, because it showed her going through a particular change that we thought was important. We exercised some selectivity.

However, even within that finite unit of time, there's more going on than we can use. Some events aren't important. Some aren't interesting. After all, we don't see Red Riding Hood doing her homework or having lunch or buying her mother a birthday card; we don't see Dorothy looking for a doggie biscuit to feed Toto, or discussing the price of straw with the Scarecrow. In both narratives, we only see those incidents that are somehow connected to the heart of the play; that is, its *dramatic action*.

Thus, out of all the possible things that could happen in a story, you choose only certain ones to show us as you fashion the play. But how do you choose which ones are in and which ones out? The kinds of choices often fall into several common categories. Let's look at what Tennessee Williams did with *The Glass Menagerie*, for example.

The Incidents All Have Something in Common

Everything in the play should somehow contribute to the overall dramatic action; that is, the incidents are related in some way to the significant change that takes place. All the incidents we see in the play contribute either directly or indirectly to Tom's decision to leave home and the feelings of guilt he has as a result. These include Laura's getting fired, Amanda's search for a Gentleman Caller and the burden it places on Tom, Amanda's preparations for the dinner, and the unfortunate consequences of the visit.

The Incidents Collectively Help Us Understand the Characters Better

In each incident we observe, we learn new and important things about Tom's personality, his relation to Laura, the kind of family environment he lives in, his feelings toward Amanda, his secret desires and dreams, his propensity to daydream, and so forth, so that we ultimately understand both why he chooses to leave and why he feels as guilty about it as he does. You'll recall the point I made when we discussed goals, obstacles, and strategies: the ones you choose always reveal character.

The Incidents Are All Related to Each Other

Each of the incidents has certain characteristics in common, or in conflict, with the others.

1. Mood

Notice how many scenes in the play involve quarrels and recriminations, and then notice how they are contrasted with scenes of calm, connection, affection. You'll find that one mood alternates with another on a fairly regular basis. What might Williams be trying to suggest by this collection?

2. Setting

Notice that all the scenes take place in the house, except for those moments on the fire escape. Observe the difference in the kinds of scenes they are: The scenes that take place inside are confrontations or plans about the Gentleman Caller, while the ones that take place on the porch are those in which characters (specifically Amanda and Tom) talk about dreams, longings, and illusions. There is a reason why scenes about escape take place on the fire escape.

3. Character Revelation

Note how many scenes show us how the characters are alike or different in important ways: Amanda constantly lives in the past, Laura in her world of music and toys, Tom at the movies. How many scenes are about somebody telling lies to somebody else or to themselves? How many scenes are about somebody shattering something somebody else holds important—whether that thing is a false dream, a lie, or a glass animal?

Only one scene brings in somebody from outside the family. What happens in this scene that's different from any other? For one thing, it puts Laura center stage, whereas she hasn't been there before. For another, it shows us Laura's only real contact with the "outside" world. For a third, it's the scene in which the most important discovery is made, the most important dream is shattered, and Laura learns how cruel the real world can be.

4. Ideas

A close examination of the content of each incident reveals that somehow they all deal with some aspect of truth versus illusion: Tom's opening monologue, Amanda's reminiscences at dinner, Amanda's discovering Laura's secret, Tom's escape to the movies and to the magic show, the frustrations over the plans for the Gentleman Caller, Amanda's pretense of richness and her plans to capture Jim, Tom's secret about the electric bill and the merchant marine, and finally, Jim's disclosure of his plans to marry Betty. All of them are about dreams of one sort or another.

The Incidents Selected Somehow Make the Story Move Forward

To explain what this involves, we must explore the second part of our definition of plot: the arrangement of the incidents.

Arrangement

How the incidents are arranged contributes greatly to the meaning of the play. You have two options in this respect. You can put the events in the order in which they occur or you can arrange them in some other sequence. We are most accustomed to the former; we are used to seeing things in both a chronological and a causal order. That is to say, incident A causes B, which in turn causes C, and that's the order we see them in. *These plays are linear and considered realistic.*

On the other hand, some plays are not realistic and do not show life in cause-and-effect terms. Because we first see incident A and then we see incident B does not mean that the second one is a result of the first one. The fact that you see me with a gun in scene 1 and you see John dead in scene 2 does not mean that I shot him.

Furthermore, the sequence of events might bounce around

in time, for whatever reason you choose. For instance, Harold Pinter's play *Betrayal* begins at the end of the story and works backward to the beginning. Or the second incident we see may not necessarily be logically related to the first; this order appears, for instance, in Eugene Ionesco's *The Bald Soprano*. Here, a fireman appears in the middle of a dinner party where there's no fire. Chronology and perhaps causality are not involved in this at all. *These plays are nonlinear and very often not realistic at all.*

As we said, the most common order is linear; it's the sort of order you are most likely to encounter in plays, especially the ones you study early on. This linear structure has, over the years, developed a unique and defining pattern; that is, we have come to expect, and playwrights have commonly written, certain kinds of incidents to happen in a certain kind of order. This pattern has become more or less standard, and when most people talk about *plot*, it is this pattern they are referencing. In the nineteenth century, a French scholar named Gustav Freytag codified and described it, and today we often refer to it as the "Freytag pyramid." You'll see why it's called a "pyramid" a bit later on. Let's find out what the structural points are and how the pyramid works.

1. State of equilibrium: This is the section in which we are first introduced to the characters, the kind of world they inhabit, and some potential problems that seem to lie just below the surface.

2. Inciting incident: Something happens to disturb the characters and/or to upset their world, throwing it, as we often say, "out of balance." In this part of the play, one character begins to attract our interest; this person then typically becomes the center of attention, the *agent of action*. We learn important things about this person: what the specific problem she faces is, what she wants to do about it, where or how she is vulnerable, and how important this task is to her.

3. Point of attack of the major dramatic question: This is the moment in which the inciting incident upsets the state of equilibrium and gives rise to the major question of plot that will drive the action for the rest of the play. See chapter 8 for a discussion of what a *major dramatic question* is.

4. Rising action: The major part of your play, this step consists of crises that occur when the *agent of action* meets an *obstacle* and has to generate some *strategy* to get around it.

5. Climax: This is the point at which the story turns in a major direction, the protagonist faces a final obstacle, and ultimate choices are made. This section often includes moments of what are called *reversal* and *recognition*, which we'll define in due course. This moment also helps define whether the plot is *simple* or *complex*, additional terms we'll define later.

6. Resolution: The consequences of what has gone before take effect, and people make new adjustments to a new situation.

7. New state of equilibrium: The world is once again at rest but is now somehow very different from what it was before.

Figure 1 shows what this pattern looks like. Now you see why it's called a pyramid.

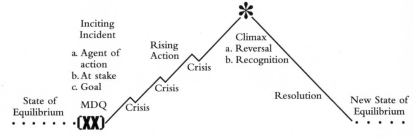

Figure 1. Freytag Pyramid

Let's explore each of these sections in a little more detail.

The State of Equilibrium

The *state of equilibrium* shows us what the world of the play is like before something happens to it. We most often learn this in the early scenes. Some of the things that are typically important are the characters, the setting, and potential trouble spots.

Who Are the Characters?

Of course, the obvious questions are: What are their names? What relationship do they have with each other? What kind of people do they seem to be?

What Kind of World Do They Live In?

Where are we? This means more than what room we happen to be in, or what house belongs to this front porch, or any other aspect of its physical location.

Where Are We in Time?

Are we in the present or in a different time?

Where Are We in Society?

What is the environment? Socially? Economically? What is there in the place that will prove important to the people?

Where Are We in the Mind?

What is the tone or mood of the place: Does it seem a safe place? A happy place? Is the world sick—as it is in *Oedipus*? Or is it delightfully wacky as it is in *The Importance of Being Earnest*?

What Potential Problems Seem to Be Bubbling beneath the Surface?

Some time very soon, something is going to come along to throw this world out of whack. The seeds of what this "something" might be are usually planted here; this is called *foreshadowing*.

In *The Glass Menagerie,* what is the state of equilibrium? We know the historical setting, because Tom spells it out for us in his opening monologue. We know the physical setting, because Tom describes it for us. And we get a sense of the psychological framework of this world when Tom tells us:

> I turn back time. I reverse it to that quaint period, the thirties, when the huge middle class of America was matriculating in a school for the blind. . . . they were having their fingers pressed forcibly down on the fiery Braille of a dissolving economy. In Spain there was revolution.

We learn in the first scene who the people are and what they're like. Amanda is a talker and the matriarch. She lives in the past. She has weird ideas about social decorum. She talks about "gentlemen callers" coming for Laura. It seems fairly obvious that Amanda lives in her dreams and has no clue what the real world is like. Laura is shy and has low self-esteem. Tom seems to be the only stable one here. We also know that they're poor, and Tom is the breadwinner.

The Inciting Incident

Trouble comes along. A problem appears. A situation arises. And somebody has to do something about it. Important things are involved here.

Where Does the Problem Come From?

Does it come from another person who somehow messes things up? Does it come from some aspect of society—money, laws, government? Does it come from the past—something long held secret that is threatened with exposure? Does it come from some flaw in somebody's character?

In *The Glass Menagerie*, what is the bad thing that comes along? In scene 2, Amanda learns that Laura has dropped out of business school. She's not bringing in any money, but much more importantly, she is not learning any skills that will help her survive in the world when Amanda is gone. Who will take care of her?—she obviously can't take care of herself. In Amanda's society, single old maids are treated brutally and lead awful lives—she can't stand the thought of Laura becoming one. Note that, in this play, the inciting incident has actually happened before the curtain goes up. However, it's Amanda's learning of it that effectively changes Amanda's world.

Who Is Most Affected by the Problem? Who Has to Do Something to Solve It?

Clearly, Amanda. She has to find some way to help Laura develop survival skills. Therefore, it's Amanda who emerges as the play's agent of action.

What Is She Going to Do? What Becomes Her Goal?

Amanda makes it clear: she'll have to find Laura a husband.

Take a moment to review chapter 3 on goals; apply the requirements of well-chosen goals to Amanda's. You'll note that all the essentials are here:

1. It's specific and visible: Laura must get married.

2. It's completable: It will end when Laura says, "I do."

3. It's positive: Amanda is going toward something, not leaving something.

4. It certainly is important. The stakes are very high: survival.

5. It certainly involves somebody else: Tom, Laura, and the prospective bridegroom.

What Emerges as the Major Dramatic Question?

Tom tells it as clearly as can be in the narration before scene 3:

> After the failure at Rubicam's Business College, the idea of getting a gentleman caller for Laura began to play a more and more important part in Mother's calculations. It became an obsession.

We can state it as, "Will Amanda get a husband for Laura?" What follows immediately, of course, is that Amanda begins to apply her first strategy: convincing Tom to bring home a gentleman caller for Laura. (Although in this play, there is only one strategy: when Gentleman Caller Jim proves a dead end, Williams ends the play. Perhaps he is suggesting there is no other strategy available to Amanda.)

Rising Action: Crises

As you can tell from the diagram, this section forms the bulk of the play and consists of a series of crises. By definition, a *crisis* is a moment in the play when something happens to make a difference in the agent of action's actions. We might also say that it's any moment in the rising action when an obstacle forces a new strategy. It also helps if you think of the moment as a "turning point," when the play shifts direction. It's during this step that the various interconnected strategies appear.

Let's explore some of what Tennessee Williams has done. In scene 2, the first of many crises appears when Amanda finds out that Laura has not been going to school. Yes, it's true: we have already identified this moment as the inciting incident, but it's still a crisis. It is essentially the first one. In scene 3, Tom and Amanda have a fight. Since Amanda needs Tom to help her find a gentleman caller, this fight poses an obstacle. It's that moment in the in-order-to chart we discussed in chapter 5 that involves a "however." She has to develop a side-strategy for making up with him before she can proceed. We see how she does that in scene 4, when she learns that Tom is unhappy and wants a better life. She pleads with him: "As soon as Laura has got somebody to take care of her . . .—why then you'll be free to go wherever you please." In scene 5, we learn that this side-strategy has worked: Tom announces that he's bringing a friend from work to meet Laura. This is another crisis—except that it's a good one.

Amanda now embarks on a series of sub-strategies designed to make the upcoming dinner as wonderful as she can. She chooses the right menu, she cleans, she decorates, she puts "Gay Deceivers" in Laura's dress, she does everything she can think of, according to the world that she knows.

In scene 6, the doorbell rings and Amanda tells Laura to open it for Jim, the caller. Crisis: Laura refuses (obstacle). Amanda bullies her (strategy). It works. They then sit down to dinner. Two important crises appear now—one involves the lights and one involves Laura. Can you spot them?

And we now come to the next step in the Freytag pyramid.

Climax

Climax is a hard term to define, since it involves so many possible things. Some call it the moment of highest tension, when the final outcome of the major dramatic question is on the line. Whatever happens now will bring either victory or defeat. Some call it the moment when the question is answered once and for all. Once a decision is made or a step taken, there is no turning back.

Some call it the *obligatory scene*—that moment the audience has been essentially waiting for all along—when the agent of action faces off the major obstacle for a last showdown; when the forces or ideas that have been in opposition are forced to deal directly with each other. Clearly, in *The Glass Menagerie,* the scene between Laura and Jim, the Gentleman Caller, meets both of these definitions. Laura's fate will be decided in this moment we've been anticipating since scene 3.

Aristotle doesn't give this moment a name, but he does describe what happens in it. He uses the terms *reversal* and *recognition*. By *reversal*, he means any moment in which what is happening suddenly shifts. We've already met this term when we examined the many crises that appear in the rising action. We've also met the concept of *recognition* before: it is a moment in which the agent of action comes to know or understand something he or she didn't know before. Some news is presented, a secret is revealed, a confession is made—and the world changes.

In the best plays, for Aristotle, these two moments work together, and one often causes the other. Oedipus *recognizes* the truth about his past, and he is suddenly *changed* from king to outcast. Lear is *cast out* by his daughters and *comes to understand* that being a king does not keep you safe from being human. Othello *realizes* what an idiot he's been and *kills* himself. Plays that have both these moments at work, Aristotle calls *complex* plots. Plays in which only one, or neither, of these elements appears, he calls *simple*.

What has Mr. Williams done? Actually, several things. Laura, and then Amanda and Tom, learn that Jim is already engaged. This is a major recognition. And each of them undergoes a major reversal: Laura becomes doomed to a lonely fate; Amanda's carefully built world of illusions is shattered; Tom escapes by running away (do you recall that, earlier, we had described the central action of this play as "Tom leaving"?).

Resolution

The action winds up as characters adjust to the new situation. Sometimes characters make new and different decisions, so that we see how they have been changed: Laura "blows out [her] candles." Sometimes they form new alliances or change their relationships: Tom leaves. Sometimes their personalities have changed: Amanda now seems to have "dignity and tragic beauty." Sometimes we just don't know at all, as characters are left in limbo.

New State of Equilibrium

As the lights fade for the last time, we are left with a more or less clear indication of what this new world is like. We've gone physically from one condition to another; mentally from ignorance to knowledge; socially from one set of relationships to another; and symbolically from—well, that's up for you to decide. But, in whatever fashion you choose, *the world is different.* There has been that most important element of all: a *major change.*

Variations on the Pyramid

Nearly all realistic, well-made plays follow this pattern; in one form or another, all these steps appear. Typically, it all happens onstage; that is, the curtain rises during the state of equilibrium, and we spend a scene or two coming to know the world.

Sometimes the curtain rises after the inciting incident has already taken place, and the first couple scenes are about us catching up. We've noted that this is the case for *Glass Menagerie.* But it is also true for *Othello*: Iago's scene with Roderigo informs us that Othello has already promoted Cassio over him, that Othello has already married Desdemona, and that Roderigo is already miffed.

Sometimes the curtain rises in the middle of a rising action, and again we have to do some catching up. In *Fences* by August Wilson, Troy is already involved in several story threads: he's already fighting with his son, cheating on his wife, stealing from his brother—all in his desperate attempt to make something of his life that counts, or as he expresses it, "To beat Mr. Death."

And there are even occasional plays in which we come in at the climax and watch the story unfold backwards. Harold Pinter's *Betrayal* does this, as does Donald Marguiles's *Sight Unseen.*

The point bears repeating: In a realistic, well-made play, each of the steps of the Freytag pyramid appears in one form or another. Some steps may happen before the curtain goes up. Some steps may happen offstage. You may choose to show the steps in a nonlinear fashion. But their presence ensures that your plot will be coherent and strong.

Now, how about a couple of exercises to put theory into practice?

Exercise 6:1

Read a short play assigned by your teacher. Locate and identify the lines that make up the key steps of the Freytag pyramid.

Exercise 6:2

Prepare an outline for a twenty- to twenty-five-minute play. Describe in as much detail as you can what will happen in each of the key steps.

Revision Questions

At any point in the writing process, your responders may ask you a number of questions indicating that your plot is loosely structured or missing key points. People may be confused about shifts in the story, illogical leaps from one situation to another, vague and/or ambiguous moments of what is supposed to be tension, but only seems artificial. Things may happen too quickly. Things may happen in ways that don't lead anywhere or come from anywhere. Characters may make decisions that don't seem to be justified by previous events. People may not understand or notice what is supposed to be a climax: nothing of importance or consequence seems to happen. And so forth. Always go back to your plot and review these steps:

1. Examine your draft. Can you prepare an outline for it, as you did in Exercise 6:2 above?

2. What *inciting incident* have you chosen? Is it the best you can invent? In other words, does it come from a source that makes sense in terms of your play? Does it help reveal character?

3. Examine the incidents you've selected to appear in your play. Are they the best possible ones, in terms of what you want to do in your play? Are they alike or different in important ways? Do they help reveal character? Do they contribute to the *rising action*?

4. Examine the rising action. How do the various *crises* you've created contribute to the play? In other words, do they help reveal *character*? Do the *obstacles* come from the most appropriate source? Are the *strategies* chosen the best ones?

5. How does the *new state of equilibrium* compare to the original? Are the differences clear? Do they reveal what you want them to?

7

The Miniplay

The first part of this book examined four key elements that are involved in every plot: agent of action, goal, obstacles, and strategies. Our discussion of the Freytag pyramid uncovered how a plot is laid out over the whole course of the play: that is, how the agent of action continually uses new strategies to deal with obstacles as they appear, in order to achieve her goal.

What's important to note now is that not only do these four key elements appear over the play as a whole; they also appear within each individual moment of the play itself. Indeed, every time a crisis appears, the agent of action has to generate a new goal in order to get around it; this crisis has its own obstacles and strategies.

Also recall, when we examined goals, we noted that every single moment in a play is essentially a negotiation between two characters, in which A tries to convince B to do something. So in a real and very important sense, we can safely say that every single moment in a well-made play is a sort of small play in itself. Which is why I call it a *miniplay*.

So we are safe and logical in stating that a full-length play is really nothing so much as a series of miniplays—some long, some short—following one another in a chain that carries us from beginning to end. Again, actors know this as they search to uncover what's really going on beneath every line they speak. Let's see how this works on the smallest level possible.

I say to my friend, "Steve, please help me move this brick off my foot!" Where are the four keys? Well, clearly I am the agent of action. I want to get Steve to help me get the brick off my foot (goal). We can assume Steve is not being very helpful (obstacle) because I have to beg him (strategy).

How long does this miniplay last? Well, that depends on several factors. How easy is it to convince Steve? How stubborn is he being? If he responds to my line with "Fine, here we go," I've accomplished my goal and the miniplay is over. If, however, he says "No, never, never, never. I hate you and want to see you trapped there while the rising tide washes over your helpless body and drowns you!" then I have a slightly longer play to deal with. Because the obstacle is so hard, I may have to generate more strategies. I may have to offer him money, threaten him with my pocket knife, cry and plead for mercy, or summon my superpowers from Zeus and free myself. (However, if I try the last and Zeus says, "No, not today," I have *another* miniplay to deal with.)

Again, think of a brick house. Or a DNA chain. Both are self-contained in their own right and also part of a larger structure. Houses are made of bricks working together: organisms are made of cells containing DNA chains working together. When there's a dull moment in your play, you have done the equivalent of putting a very large marshmallow in the middle of a row of bricks on your house. So, plays are made of miniplays working together. Sometimes, as we've said, they follow each other. And sometimes one small miniplay might be buried inside a slightly larger miniplay, which in turn is inside one even larger. Let's examine in detail what they are and then see how to make them work. And let's go back to *Othello*. (All quotes are from the Pelican edition of *The Tragedy of Othello, the Moor of Venice*, edited by Russ McDonald, 2001.)

We've seen that, on one level, the entire play is about Iago's destruction of Othello. It is a complete dramatic action that takes nearly five full acts to complete. But let's look for miniplays. Look at the first few speeches of the opening scene: Iago and Roderigo are quarreling. They've previously made an arrangement by which

Iago would secure Desdemona for Roderigo. It hasn't been working out, and Roderigo wants his money back. Iago has to talk the man out of his anger and return him to their plan. The section begins with Roderigo's first line:

> Tush; never tell me! I take it much unkindly
> That thou, Iago, who hast had my purse
> As if the strings were thine, shouldst know of this.
>
> (1.1.1–3)

and ends with his last:

> What a full fortune does the thick-lips owe
> If he can carry't thus!
>
> (1.1.70)

The section is in itself a complete miniplay.

1. Iago is the agent of action.
2. His goal is to get Roderigo to calm down.
3. His chief obstacles are Roderigo's anger and stupidity.
4. His major strategy is to convince him that he (Iago) hates the Moor.

Our first miniplay: Iago calms Roderigo!

And, as soon as it's over, notice that a new one begins and runs for a few lines (1.1.70–80). It is all about Iago getting Roderigo to call Brabantio. It only takes ten lines for this miniplay to occur, but if Shakespeare wanted to, he could have extended this into a longer sequence. What other strategies might have Iago employed to get Brabantio out of bed?

Notice something very important about the above paragraph. In the miniplays we've seen so far (all two of them), the agent of action has been the same: Iago. However, in future miniplays, this will not be the case. Depending on what's happening in the moment, the agent of action can be anybody. We'll see that at times the moment is Roderigo's; later, the moment becomes Brabantio's, or the Duke's, or Othello's, or anybody else's. As long as *somebody is trying get somebody else to do something that is difficult*, your moments will be interesting.

What's the next miniplay? Iago convinces Brabantio to see whether or not Desdemona is at home (1.1.85–160). What's next? Brabantio goes offstage to check on this. While he's gone, Iago and Roderigo have some talk about their scheme (1.1.160–75). This scene is, essentially, a continuation of the miniplay begun at the opening, the one involving Iago's getting Roderigo to calm down.

Now Brabantio appears, and realizing that Desdemona has disappeared, vows to go off to find her. He does, beginning a new miniplay that's all about Brabantio finding his daughter and Othello. This miniplay ends several lines later (1.2.66). It doesn't take long and mostly happens offstage, but if Shakespeare had wanted to make a different play, he might have had Brabantio spend a whole act trying to find them and made a farce out of it.

Also notice that, while this miniplay is going on, it is temporarily interrupted by some new ones. Cassio enters (1.2.33), having been sent by the Duke to find Othello. We learn in their conversation that there is an invasion in progress and the Duke wants Othello to come to a war council. Although we haven't met the Duke, and the action has taken place offstage, there has been a miniplay going on here involving the Duke getting people to find Othello and bring him to the court.

However, you'll notice that I skipped over about two dozen lines at the beginning of scene 2. Examine them; what's going on? Iago asks about Othello's military history; he then asks if Othello is in truth married and warns him that Brabantio will certainly oppose the marriage. To this, Othello replies:

> Let him do his spite;
> My services which I have done the signory
> Shall out-tongue his complaints.
>
> (1.2.19–22)

What's going on here? I keep on saying that every moment in your play is a negotiation between A and B; and that every moment is part of some miniplay or other. If that's true, what's the miniplay in these twenty lines? Who is trying to get whom to do what?

On one level, it's fairly clear: Iago is asking Othello for information (that's exposition, folks, raising its ugly head). And it's certainly easy-going: Othello doesn't have any problem answering Iago's questions. But is there anything more *dramatic* going on?

Remember Iago's conversation with Roderigo in the preceding scene, wherein Iago vowed to destroy Othello? So is this probing seeking for anything *more* than just facts? Might Iago not be looking for Othello's weak spots? Is Iago, in fact, not already at work trying to destroy Othello, so that this miniplay is really about Iago's collecting materials with which to build his engine of destruction? Then what sort of miniplay do these twenty lines give us? It's not as self-sustained as others we've met so far: It began in the preceding scene and really doesn't finish until act 5, when Othello is dead.

But let's move on. Skipping ahead to scene 2, line 66: Brabantio has returned; he's found Othello, which, as we noted before, brings that little miniplay to a finish. Over the next several lines, there are several very small miniplays, all of which involve exchanges of information: Othello decides not to hide but goes into the house for some business; Iago informs Cassio about the marriage; Othello stops a sword fight between Brabantio and Iago.

However, in scene 3 an extremely important miniplay begins. Can you spot it? Find Brabantio's line (1.3.90). Here he sets out to complete a very major goal of his own: "I'll have it disputed on." And note, this is important: The rest of act 1 is basically that miniplay, in which the agent of action is Brabantio himself.

- His *goal*: Trying to annul the marriage of Desdemona to Othello.
- His *obstacles*: The reputation Othello has in Venice. The fact that Othello is a general and Venice needs him in its current war.
- His *strategies*: Take Othello to the ducal court; make his case; convince the Duke to make Othello describe his wooing of Desdemona; and convince the Duke to fetch Desdemona herself and ask her where her allegiance lies.

And note, without beating you over the head with the point, how many miniplays are inside *this*. Each of the strategies listed above makes up a small one of its own. Remember, sometimes a miniplay may be merely two lines of dialogue long, but the four keys are there.

Now that you know what Brabantio's miniplay is and where it begins, can you locate the line on which it ends? When does Brabantio's little curtain come down? It's all the way over on scene 3, line 209. What is it that Brabantio actually says? He can't be any clearer than that.

And what happens after that? Are we out of miniplays? Do new ones begin? Do old ones return? A quick examination of the rest of act 1 reveals:

- As far as we know, Roderigo is still a little mad at Iago, so the miniplay about Iago consoling (and ultimately duping) Roderigo is still in the air.
- We know that the war is still on; and the Duke is still hoping to hire Othello. Shakespeare now brings this miniplay forward.
- There's one about the Duke ultimately getting Othello to say yes.
- There's one about the Duke deciding what to do with Desdemona.
- There's a brief one about Brabantio warning Othello to watch out for Desdemona's trickery.
- Then there's a return to the miniplay that began the act: Iago finally convincing Roderigo to "put money in thy purse" and follow them all to Cyprus.

Exercise 7:1

Examine the opening pages of act 2. What happens to the miniplay about Othello defeating the invading army?

How does Shakespeare continue to use the running miniplay involving Iago and Roderigo throughout the rest of this same scene?

Examine all of act 2, scene 2. It's not very long, but it does contain a miniplay—it happens offstage, true, but it happens nevertheless. What is that miniplay?

What are the miniplays that happen between the following lines in the rest of the play?

1. Act 2, scene 1, lines 210–80, involving Iago and Roderigo
2. Act 2, scene 3, lines 58–110, involving Iago and Cassio
3. Act 3, scene 3, line 1 (This is a tricky one: notice that a very important miniplay has happened offstage between scenes 2 and 3 that involves Cassio and Desdemona. What was it?)

4. Act 3, scene 3, lines 35–88, involving Desdemona, Othello, and Iago

5. Act 4, scene 1, lines 212–73, involving Lodovico, Cassio, Othello, Desdemona, and Iago

6. Act 5, scene 2, lines 1–90, involving Desdemona and Othello

7. Act 5, scene 2, lines 281–354, from the entrance of Lodovico to Othello's suicide

Miniplays and Exposition

Now, how does this translate into your improving your play? Simply put, you must make sure that at every moment the four key ingredients are always present in one way or another. When somebody wants something and goes after it—even the smallest goal—the audience is engaged in watching an important event taking place in which the outcome may be in doubt.

This is particularly true for scenes loaded with important exposition. A scene of people exchanging information is static; but the struggle of somebody who wants something from somebody else and is having trouble getting it, that is dynamic. Go back to the opening of *Othello* for a moment, and notice how cleverly Shakespeare turns what could be a boring scene of exposition into a miniplay. The very first speech tells us that Roderigo is annoyed; Iago spends the next few moments *not* explaining things to him, but trying to calm him down. The "explanation" is not the scene, but a strategy within the scene.

RODERIGO
> Tush! never tell me; I take it much unkindly
> That thou, Iago, who hast had my purse
> As if the strings were thine, shouldst know of this.

IAGO
> 'Sblood, but you will not hear me:
> If ever I did dream of such a matter, Abhor me.

RODERIGO
> Thou told'st me thou didst hold him in thy hate.

IAGO
> Despise me, if I do not. Three great ones of the city,
> In personal suit to make me his lieutenant,
> Off-capp'd to him.

Miniplays and Stage Fillers

Here is another moment early in the play in which Shakespeare uses a miniplay to keep alive a scene that might otherwise be deadly dull. At the beginning of act 2, we learn that a severe storm has separated Othello from the rest of the fleet. Iago is waiting with some gentlemen for word, when Cassio comes to reveal that Desdemona and the ladies are safe, but no word yet about Othello. Desdemona enters right after that and sends a messenger down to the docks to see if there's any news. The scene settles into what is essentially a time-filler: while we're waiting for the messenger to return, *something* has to happen onstage to keep us interested.

What does Shakespeare do? He has Emilia, Iago, and Desdemona start to talk idle high-comedy flirtatious chatter, until Desdemona throws a challenge to Iago: "What wouldst thou write of me, if thou shouldst praise me?" Iago protests:

> O gentle lady, do not put me to't;
> For I am nothing, if not critical.

Desdemona convinces him to try:

> Come on assay. There's one gone to the harbour? . . . I am not merry; but I do beguile the thing I am, by seeming otherwise. Come, how wouldst thou praise me?
>
> (2.1.120)

What is this exchange but a miniplay?

   1. The *agent of action* is Desdemona.
   2. Her *goal* is to convince Iago to flirt with her.
   3. The *obstacle* is his reluctance.
   4. Her *strategy* is to let him know that she needs some distraction while waiting for word about her husband.

And Iago gives in. Desdemona achieves her minigoal:

> IAGO
>   I am about it; but indeed my invention
>   Comes from my pate as birdlime does from frieze;
>   It plucks out brains and all: but my Muse labours,

And thus she is deliver'd.
If she be fair and wise, fairness and wit,
The one's for use, the other useth it.

(2.1.125–30)

Revision Questions

When you hear comments such as these on your working drafts, the problem may lie with your use of miniplays.

At times I found my attention wandering; I stopped being interested. It seems to drift now and then.

It was too much talk. Sometimes, the whole scene just revolved around getting in one cool line or a silly joke. A lot was unnecessary.

Ask yourself:

1. Have you examined each key moment in your play that you have identified as static or dull, or exposition-heavy, to see whether or not the keys are at work?

2. Can you add elements to these moments to make them more dramatic? Do they function adequately as miniplays? (Keep in mind that the agent of action of the miniplay does not have to be the agent of action of the whole play. We've seen above how small moments are driven by Roderigo, the Duke, and Brabantio.)

3. Can you raise the stakes a bit or provide a harder obstacle?

4. How soon after one miniplay is over does a new one begin? If you have a stage wait of more than five lines or so, you're getting dull.

Things still a little dull? Go on to the next chapter, on *dramatic questions*, and see what that has to offer.

8

Dramatic Questions

Using miniplays as building blocks will keep your scenes from being static and passive. Keep in mind that the four keys are *always* important elements. This chapter deals with another, and closely related, concept that can also help.

What Are Dramatic Questions?

To understand this new concept, let's make a short classroom visit.

When I teach this material to my students, I face them and say, in an extremely serious tone, "I am now going to teach you the single most important element of playwriting. Are you ready?" I wait about thirty seconds and then ask, "There. Did you get it?"

Of course, they are confused. And so I do it again. "I am now going to teach you the single most important element of playwriting" And after a long pause, "Did you get it?"

By now they are lost. I then ask them to think back to those moments of empty silence and try to recall what was happening to them during the pause. After some discussion, we agree that those silences weren't empty after all. They were filled with suspense and anticipation.

The lesson is simple: the single most important element is suspense, making the audience anxious to pay close attention to the action in order to find out what comes next. However, we're still a bit off the mark. The question still remains: Suspense about what? Anticipation for what? And, most important, how do you create it?

I then ask my students to think again about exactly what was going on in their heads during that minute. Eventually, my students realize that the pause wasn't silent after all. Actually, a wide range of questions was going through their minds. They were asking themselves all sorts of things. I ask them to list the questions:

1. What is the secret?
2. What's he doing?
3. Why is he doing this?
4. Does he know? Is he serious or just fooling around?
5. Where is this going?
6. Did I miss something?
7. Will he tell us?

And so forth, with many variations on these—some of them a little unprintable. Once this list is up, I draw their attention to the fact that what I have just done is what playwrights always do: I create suspense and anticipation in the audience by *raising questions in their minds, creating a desire* for them to know the answers, and then *delaying giving them the answer* as long as possible. And, because these questions are always related to some dramatic situation, I label them generically as *dramatic questions*. And this indeed *is* the single most important element in playwriting and bears restating: Raising questions in the minds of the audience, creating a desire to know the answer, and delaying the revelation of the answer as long as you can.

Once this concept is clear, I return to the list on the chalkboard and draw my students' attention to two very important factors:

1. *The most interesting questions are those that begin with an interrogative pronoun or adverb: what, why, where, and so on.* Look at the list above, and see if you can rewrite those that don't. For instance, number 4 could become, "What is his real intention here?," and number 6, "What did I miss?"

2. *These questions fall into two major categories.* Examine them carefully and see if you can spot what they are. Some of the questions are about *information* (1, 2, 3, 4, 5, 6) and others are about action, or *plot* (7).

Questions of Information

The first group of questions are those that seek information in their answer. *What* is he doing? *Why* is he doing this? *Who* is he? *What* has happened offstage? And so forth. The answer to these questions is always a fact of some sort: She's doing this. He's here because he's hungry. She's going to the store. He's my brother. Grandma just got run over by a reindeer. The answer is a fact. Let's give this category a name: *questions of information*, or QI's. Let's define it as *questions raised in the minds of an audience that have a fact as an answer*.

This is a very broad category and includes a wide range of questions. All but one of the questions on the board have been of this sort. Most often, the answers to these questions come in the form of exposition, about which we will have more to say in chapter 10. Questions of information, therefore, are the first category. What's the second? Did you notice, by the way, that when I wrote that last sentence, I raised in your mind a—what? Yes, a question of information.

Questions of Plot

The second category of dramatic questions is exemplified by number 7, "Where is this going?," or some variation thereof, in which the question asks not about a fact, but about a course of action in the future. Such questions raise in our minds curiosity about the event to come, the series of steps that are going to be undertaken, and very often the nature of the outcome. In short, this category deals with the story itself and therefore is aptly labeled *questions of plot*; we'll define it as *questions raised in the minds of an audience that have* the outcome of a course of action *as an answer*.

Think of it this way: Often people claim that the difference between a play and a novel is that a play takes place in the present, while a novel takes place in the past. Actually, both are untrue. Any effective narrative takes place in only one dimension: the future. Or rather, the expectation of the future. We don't care so much about what happened *then*, nor are we that much concerned about what's happening *now*. What really keeps us in suspense is wondering what's going to happen *next*— be that the next five minutes or the next two years. Questions of plot do this: They set up our concerns for later and take us into the future. Most often, they are answered by a simple "yes" or "no," depending on what happens at the end of the story.

Here are some examples of questions of plot: If I give you the question, can you identify the play?

1. *Will* this young man revenge his father's death?
2. *Will* this woman find a husband for her daughter?
3. *Will* this king solve the mystery which happened years ago?
4. *Will* this tired salesman get his boss to give him a job in the store and take him off the road?
5. *Will* this handsome young man finally marry the pretty heiress?
6. *Will* this villain succeed in getting the general to destroy himself?

(Answers: *Hamlet, The Glass Menagerie, Oedipus Rex, Death of a Salesman,* any romantic comedy you can think of, and, of course, *Othello.*)

Now try the reverse. Here are some titles. Can you think of the question of plot that runs through each play?

1. *A Doll's House*
2. *The Importance of Being Earnest*
3. *Romeo and Juliet*
4. *Antigone*
5. *Fences*

Your answers might look like these:

1. Will Nora manage to escape the clutches of Krogstad?
2. Will Jack manage to marry Gwendolyn?
3. Will Romeo manage to live with Juliet in marriage?
4. Will Antigone get away with civil disobedience?
5. Will Troy get away with lying?

Questions of plot essentially are the prime movers of your play, continually generating suspense. Making the audience wonder about a fact raises their curiosity, but making them wonder about the *outcome of an action* keeps them engaged.

Okay. You understand the difference between the two kinds of questions. Now it gets a little more complicated. We need to say a few more things about questions of plot.

1. There Are Two Distinct Kinds of Questions of Plot

While both kinds of questions of plot are about whether or not something will happen, sometimes they involve an outcome that plays out right here and right now as we watch. Will I get you to pick up that piece of paper? Will I get you to answer my question? Will I get you to lend me five dollars? These are *immediate* outcomes; and we can refer to these kinds of questions as *minor dramatic questions of plot*. We'll refer to these from now on by a lowercase abbreviation: qp's. They typically drive the moment, or the scene. Or, since you've just learned a useful and important concept in the previous chapter, we can safely say that an immediate qp is the one that runs through whatever small and specific miniplay we are currently in.

Here are some examples, from scenes we've already examined. Go back to the discussion of the opening act of *Othello* and note what miniplays you discovered. What minor qp's does each contain?

- Will Iago succeed in calming down Roderigo?
- Will Iago get Roderigo to call out Brabantio?
- Will Brabantio find his daughter?
- Will Brabantio get the Duke to annul the marriage?
- Will Othello agree to take over the army?
- Will the Duke allow Othello to take Desdemona with him to Cyprus?

Note that that some of these qp's are answered within one or two lines; some are not answered for a page or two. They are still comparatively *immediate*.

On the other hand, sometimes the question of plot concerns an outcome that will happen in *the near or distant future*. Will I get you to pass this course? Will I succeed in becoming chairman of the board? Will I eventually solve the murder or not? These are *long-range* outcomes; and we can label these as *major dramatic questions of plot*. They typically drive the overall play itself. (We'll refer to these from now on with an abbreviation in uppercase letters: QP's.)

In summary, a question of plot can be immediate (qp) or long-range (QP).

2. Every Question of Plot Is an Interrogative Sentence That Has a Subject

Nora, Jack, Romeo, Antigone, and Troy: If you think about it, you'll realize that these people turn out to be the agents of action of the plays or the miniplays they are in.

- Will *Iago* succeed in calming down Roderigo?
- Will *Iago* get Roderigo to call out Brabantio?
- Will *Brabantio* find his daughter?
- Will *Brabantio* get the Duke to annul the marriage?

Let me restate here a point I made in the previous chapter: the agent of action of the miniplay—or as we rephrase the concept here, the "subject" of the qp—is not always the same person who drives the whole play. Each miniplay has its own agent of action; each qp has its own subject.

3. Every Question of Plot Has an Outcome Implied

In other words, the answer to the question involves some action being finished; something is accomplished. This might mean escaping the villain's clutches, marrying Gwendolyn, living with Juliet, and so on. If you review chapters 3 and 6, you'll quickly realize that the matter of goals comes to the forefront here. Every miniplay involves a quest, and you can't have a quest without a goal. Again, some of these goals might be attainable within seconds; some might take hours; some might never be attained at all—but they still drive the play.

So, to summarize so far:

1. We've looked at two kinds of dramatic questions: questions of *information* and questions of *plot*.

2. There are two kinds of questions of plot: *minor* questions (qp's), which deal with the current miniplay on stage, and *major* questions (QP's), which deal with long-range questions of the whole play.

3. Minor questions of plot are linked to the miniplays they drive. As I mentioned at the start of this chapter, the two concepts are essentially two sides of the same coin.

Questions of Character

Now, at the risk of thoroughly confusing you, I am going to introduce an actual *third* kind of dramatic question. This kind of question usually happens very late in the play, which is why I've saved it until last.

Typically, a well-made play's major question of plot (QP) leads us through the course of the action to the final outcome, which happens at the climax, and the answer is a definite "yes" or "no." Nora does escape Krogstad's clutches. Jack does manage to marry Gwendolyn. Iago has managed to get Othello to kill himself. But Romeo does not manage to live with Juliet in marriage, Antigone clearly does not get away with civil disobedience, and Laura remains completely not engaged to be married. The action as such is over.

However, the play itself may not be. There are still some things up in the air; and one of those important things is how the agent of action will deal with this final answer. How has the character been changed by the outcome? What has Nora learned? Is Jack happy with the news? How does Romeo handle Juliet's death? How will Antigone face her ultimate fate? What will Othello do now that he's realized the truth? And how will Laura live out the rest of her life?

What we in the audience essentially ask now becomes a *question of character* (QC), which can be phrased in several different ways:

- How has the main agent of action been changed?
- What important new element in the agent's character might emerge now?
- What will this person do from here on out? How will his or her life be different?

And so forth.

If you're observant here, you'll notice that this last category is essentially another form of question of information, since it asks "what" or "how." And yes, essentially it is true: a QC is a very special type of QI.

Any great play you know will raise one of these questions at the end, although it may not always answer it. Once we see that Macbeth is never going to stay king, we then watch how he handles the rest of his life. Once we realize that this Gentleman Caller is not going to marry Laura, we watch as Amanda comforts her and becomes visibly stronger and more nurturing. We see before our eyes that one important thing all plays must have: *change.*

An Extended Example

Okay, now you know in theory what keeps the audience in suspense. Let's spend a little more time with *Othello* and see what these various questions actually look like in a great drama. We'll see how Shakespeare uses them and then talk about how you can use them to improve your second draft.

Let's begin with the biggie: On the largest scale, what is the key *major question of plot* that runs through the whole play; that one question often referred to as the *major dramatic question* (MDQ)? Shakespeare makes it very clear in act 1, scene 3. Not only does he spell out Iago's goal but also begins to hint at his major strategies:

> To get his [Cassio's] place and to plume up my will
> In double knavery—How, how? Let's see:—
> After some time, to abuse Othello's ear
> That he is too familiar with his wife.
> He hath a person and a smooth dispose
> To be suspected—framed to make women false.
> The Moor is of a free and open nature,
> That thinks men honest that but seem to be so,
> And will as tenderly be led by the nose
> As asses are.
> I have't.
> It is engender'd. Hell and night
> Must bring this monstrous birth to the world's light.

The QP couldn't be any clearer: Will Iago get Cassio's place and "plume up his will"? But wait, you may say to yourself. There's something wrong here, isn't there? All this time we've been talking as though Iago's goal was to destroy Othello. Here, however, he states that it is to get Cassio's job: Iago says nothing about getting Othello to kill himself. Critics have questioned this seeming inconsistency: Iago says one thing but does another. Several answers have been proposed: that Iago is only lying here, to himself and us; that Iago begins with one goal but then gets so caught up in his scheme that the other goal takes over; or that Shakespeare himself, in the heat of composition, was just being careless. A possible solution lies in Iago's ambiguous phrase "double knavery." Hate to say it, folks, but Shakespeare's a little too vague here; perhaps he should have read chapter 3 on goals and rewritten the speech.

Be that as it may, let's examine the play in more detail. Let's return to the level of the miniplay again, and see, line-by-line for a while, how Shakespeare uses dramatic questions to keep our interest. We'll take the beginning of the play again, since we're already familiar with it.

Keep in mind that we're in the audience now; we're not reading a script, so we have no stage directions to help us.

The curtain goes up. Two men enter.	QUESTION RAISED
	QI-1: Who are these men?
One of them speaks:	QUESTIONS RAISED
Tush! never tell me; I take it much unkindly	
That thou, Iago, who hast had my purse	QI-2: What are they quarreling about?
As if the strings were thine, shouldst know of this.	QI-3: What is the "this" he's referring to?
	QUESTION ANSWERED
	QI-1: One of them is named Iago.
The one named Iago speaks:	
'Sblood, but you will not hear me:	QUESTION RAISED
If ever I did dream of such a matter, Abhor me.	qp-1: Will Iago get the other to hear him? (Note that this marks the beginning of a miniplay about Iago calming

The other one speaks.
Thou told'st me thou didst
    hold him in thy hate.

IAGO
Despise me if I do not. Three
    great ones of the city,
In personal suit to make me
    his lieutenant,
Off-capped to him; and, by the
    faith of man,
I know my price; I am worth no
    worse a place.
But he, as loving his own pride
    and purposes
Evades them with a bombast
    circumstance
Horribly stuff'd with epithets
    of war;

Nonsuits my mediators; for,
    "Certes," says he,
"I have already chose my officer."
And what was he?
Forsooth, a great arithmetician,
One Michael Cassio, a Florentine,
(A fellow almost damn'd in a
    fair wife;)
. . .
But he, sir, had the election:

Roderigo down. As we read
further, keep this miniplay
in mind and note when it
ends. This is a trick question.)

QUESTIONS RAISED
We still don't know the other
    man's name; when does
    Shakespeare answer this ques-
    tion? Read on.

QI-4: Who is the "him" he is
talking about?

QUESTIONS RAISED
Several small QIs are raised
    here, but in each case, Iago
    answers them right away; e.g.,
    we know immediately all we
    need to know about a man
    named Cassio.

And I (of whom his eyes had
   seen the proof
At Rhodes, at Cyprus and
   on other grounds
Christian and heathen) must be
   be-leed and calmd
By debtor and creditor. This
   counter-caster,
He, in good time, must his
   lieutenant be,
And I—God bless the mark!—
   his Moorship's ancient.

QI-3 and QI-4 are still unanswered, although we get a
mysterious clue in a moment
when the "him" is referred
to as "his Moorship." Our
interest is certainly aroused.

QUESTION ANSWERED
QI-1: We learn a little more
   about Iago. He is the "Moorship's ancient."

The other man speaks: By heaven,
   I rather would have been
   his hangman.

The miniplay continues for another twenty lines or so. Notice that it is still riding on the qp "Will Iago get the other man to calm down?" For the moment, there is no other qp in the air. Now, skip ahead to line 60: what QI is answered when Iago says, "It is as sure as you are Roderigo"?

By now, you may have noticed that the play's getting a little dull. Shakespeare's gotten about as much mileage out of the current qp-1 as he can. It's time to raise another one and begin another miniplay. As you might recall from the previous chapter, he does so on line 66:

IAGO
Call up her father,
Rouse him. Make after him,
   poison his delight,
Proclaim him in the streets.
   Incense her kinsmen,

QUESTIONS RAISED
QI-5: Whom does "her"
   refer to?
QI-6: Who is "her father"?
   We do not know who
   these people are, but they

And, though he in a fertile
climate dwell,
Plague him with flies.

. . .

RODERIGO
Here is her father's house; I'll
call aloud.

IAGO
Do, with like timorous accent
and dire yell
As when, by night and negligence,
the fire
Is spied in populous cities.

RODERIGO
What, ho, Brabantio! Signor
Brabantio, ho!

IAGO
Awake! What, ho, Brabantio!
Thieves! Thieves! Thieves!
Look to your house, your
daughter and your bags!
Thieves! Thieves!

are generating a lot of attention.
qp-2: Will Iago get Roderigo
to "call up her father"? A new
miniplay begins. Also notice
that the qp of Iago calming
Roderigo down is still in the
air. Is this line, therefore, a
new strategy on Iago's part to
get Roderigo off his back?

QUESTION ANSWERED
qp-2: The miniplay is over, as
Roderigo immediately starts
calling.
QI-6: Now we know "her"
father is named Brabantio.
QUESTION RAISED
qp-3: Will Iago and Roderigo
get Brabantio to appear?

Note, for the fun of it, that Shakespeare might have extended
the qp-2 miniplay a while. For instance, Roderigo might have
been reluctant to call out the man; he might have been afraid,
or he might have had another idea in mind. Perhaps Iago would
have had to threaten, cajole, or insist. Had Shakespeare chosen
this route, we would have learned a little more about Iago and
Roderigo right away, but the play might have been a little stalled.

In the above qp's, please observe how I have phrased each of the questions to make it involve somebody getting somebody else to do something. In the above, for instance, it was *not* "Will Roderigo call her father?"; and here, is it *not* "Will Brabantio appear?" Remember that every moment in a play is a negotiation between two people; a scene in which A tries to convince B to do something. Refer to chapter 3 on goals and how they often require another person to help complete.

A stage direction tells us "BRABANTIO *appears at a window.*"

But remember, we in the audience do not have programs. We don't know who this man is. For the moment, a new QI might be raised ("Who is this man?"), but because he's answering to the name "Brabantio," who we know is this woman's father, we can assume it is Brabantio.
QUESTION ANSWERED

BRABANTIO
What is the reason of this terrible summons?
What is the matter there?

qp-3: Here he is. Another miniplay has begun and ended very quickly. Had Shakespeare wanted to, he could have extended this one and made it harder to get the old man to appear. How?
QUESTIONS RAISED
QI-7: It's in the line: What's the reason for this summons?
qp-4: Will Brabantio get Roderigo and Iago to tell him what's going on?

Like Brabantio, we in the audience still don't know what's going on. All we know is that two men have been quarreling, they've referred to somebody as "his Moorship," and mentioned a "her." Shakespeare has taken great care to suck us into the middle of a quarrel and make us curious to see how it works itself out, but we still don't have the details yet. Is this good writing? How bored are you? Still interested to know what's coming?

Read through the following lines, and notice that Brabantio actually has trouble getting the other men to tell him what this is all about. Observe how both men tease him with mysterious questions, drop ominous hints, use a few obscene jokes, and so on. Along the way, several QI's are raised about what's happening, as are several very small qp's. I'll give you hints where they start and end, but see if you can phrase them yourself. Ultimately, when Brabantio succeeds—when this little miniplay is over—we'll feel as though something important has happened.

RODERIGO	QI starts. qp ends.
Signior, is all your family within?	
IAGO	QI starts. qp ends.
Are your doors locked?	
BRABANTIO	QI starts. qp starts.
Why, therefore, ask you this?	
IAGO	
'Zounds, sir, you're robbed!	
For shame, put on your gown!	
Your heart is burst, you have	
lost half your soul.	
Even now, now, very now, an	
old black ram	
Is topping your white ewe.	
Arise, arise!	
Awake the snorting citizens	
with the bell,	
Or else the devil will make a	
grandsire of you.	
Arise, I say!	Some QI's are answered, others
BRABANTIO	raised; qp's still unanswered.
What, have you lost your wits?	

RODERIGO

Most reverend signior, do you
    know my voice?

BRABANTIO

Not I. What are you?

RODERIGO

My name is Roderigo.

BRABANTIO

The worser welcome!
I have charged thee not to haunt
    about my doors.

QI starts; qp starts.

QI starts; qp starts.

Examine the rest of the sequence, through line 130. Most of this miniplay, as you've seen, centers on the qp, "Will Brabantio get them to tell him what's going on?" However, it is interrupted—that is, the answer is delayed—by smaller qp's that digress from the main issue. Will Roderigo get Brabantio to listen to him? Will Brabantio get Roderigo to stop pestering him? At one point, Iago enters the fray with a qp: Will Iago get Brabantio to pay attention to what's going on?

Eventually, things calm down enough, so that on line 118, Iago can begin to tell Brabantio what's happened:

> . . . But, I beseech you,
> If't be your pleasure and most wise consent,
> As partly I find it is, that your fair daughter,
> At this odd-even and dull watch o' the night,
> Transported, with no worse nor better guard
> But with a knave of common hire, a gondolier,
> To the gross clasps of a lascivious Moor—
> If this be known to you and your allowance,
> We then have done you bold and saucy wrong.
> But if you know not this, my manners tell me
> We have your wrong rebuke.

We've had about fifteen minutes of qp's about a variety of things, an interweaving of miniplays that have been small power struggles, and a collection of QI's both answered and not answered. And it's only now that we actually find out what's going on. We know who the Moor is and what he's done. We know who this "her" is and how Brabantio is connected to her. We're up to speed.

And what does Shakespeare have to do right now? Remember, the more time that passes without some question of plot in the air, the more static the play becomes. How soon is a new qp raised? Turn to line 135:

IAGO
    Straight satisfy yourself.
    If she be in your chamber or your house . . .

In response to this challenge (qp), Brabantio calls out for light to see by. A miniplay happens offstage. While it goes on, what is happening onstage? What qp is raised between Iago and Roderigo?

Clearly Iago continues to mollify Roderigo, offering him more confidential information as his strategy. He affirms he hates the Moor. At the very end of their scene, Shakespeare raises a very specific qp, on line 156, which sends us directly into the future:

IAGO
    Lead to the Sagittary the raised search;
    And there will I be with him. Farewell.

So we know that a scheme is started, trouble is in the air. We know there's some tension between Iago and Roderigo over a woman, and we know that this woman has married a Moor and that her father is not happy. Are there any qp's in the air? While there are still several unanswered QI's, the only qp is about meeting at the Sagittary. How soon does Shakespeare raise another? When's the next miniplay started and what is it?

It's in Brabantio's hands. He comes back in, affirming that his daughter is gone—answering several QIs. He's distressed and confused. He announces several qp's:

- Call up my brother. (173)
- Do you know where we may apprehend her? (174)
- At every house I'll call; / I may command at most. (178/179)

And away he goes, sending Roderigo off.

And we end scene 1 with a very important qp in the air: "Will Brabantio succeed in apprehending his daughter?"

What happens next? Examine the rest of the act on your own, and notice how Shakespeare uses dramatic questions throughout.

- At the beginning of scene 2, we finally meet this man they've been speaking of, this Moor named Othello. Key QI's are answered.
- But several new and crucial QI's are raised about the current situation in Venice: the impending war, the truth of Othello's marriage; the steps that Brabantio might take, and so on.
- Cassio and others come to find Othello to take him to the Duke. Several qp's and miniplays about this: Will Othello go? Will he agree to their requests? Will he do anything about Brabantio, and so on.
- Brabantio appears in scene 2, line 75, and declares his goal: "I'll have it disputed upon." As you'll recall from the last chapter, this qp eventually becomes the driving force of the rest of this act. Act 1 is, for all structural purposes, a play about Brabantio!

Hopefully by now you've come to see how dramatic questions keep your play from becoming static. By making the audience wonder about facts, people, and events, you continue to hold their interest and make things important. After all, notice that Shakespeare begins his play with Iago and Roderigo. He doesn't introduce Othello to us until a very tense dramatic situation has already been set up. He wants us to understand first who Othello is, why he's important, what he's done, and who his enemies are. He wants us to see Othello operating in a world that is seething with danger and potential conflict. In order to do that, he takes us through a variety of miniplays, each with its own set of dramatic questions, each compelling in its own way.

Exercise 8:1

In chapter 7, I challenged you to locate the action in the miniplays that take place in the following scenes. Go back to them again; this time, can you spot the exact line at which a specific question of plot is raised? Is this a qp for the miniplay, or is it a QP that extends into the future? I'll help you with the first one:

1. Act 2, scene 1, lines 210–80, between Iago and Roderigo: When Iago says, "Let thy soul be instructed," he's raising a qp for the scene, but when he says, "Do you find some occasion to anger Cassio?," he's projecting us into the future.
2. Act 2, scene 3, lines 58–110, between Iago and Cassio
3. Act 3, scene 3, line 1. This was a tricky one: notice that a very important miniplay has happened offstage between these two scenes. It involves Cassio and Desdemona:. But what qp do we begin the new scene with?
4. Act 3, scene 3, lines 35–88, involving Desdemona, Othello, and Iago
5. Act 4, scene 1, lines 212–73 involving Lodovico, Cassio, Othello, and Iago
6. Act 5, scene 2, lines 1–90, involving Desdemona and Othello
7. Act 5, scene 2, lines 281–354

Questions of Character

Before we leave this chapter and our dissection of the play, we do need to find examples of the third kind of dramatic question: that of *character*. Remember that these questions are typically raised after moments of intense climax, and they are often the result of answers to long-range questions of plot: that is, when your agent of action finally wins or loses, what does he or she turn into?

Brabantio provides one example. Locate act 1, scene 3, line 189. Brabantio has been fighting to annul the marriage and now realizes he has lost. Notice how quickly and diplomatically he gives in. He has become resigned, an interesting character trait.

Ah, but now look down at line 292; what little twist of the knife does Brabantio get in here? A little planting of suspicion? A little unfair play? A little sour loser becoming evident?

Othello provides another. Locate act 5, scene 2, line 356. When he learns the ultimate truth, what sort of man does Othello become? Is his suicide honorable or cowardly? Is it a sign of remorse or a act of an idiot? Something has happened; you decide what.

Iago provides a third. Locate act 5, scene 2, line 303–305. When Iago's treachery has been discovered and the truth is out, what sort of man does he turn into? What do you make of his vow of perpetual silence?

Using Dramatic Questions

This chapter has taken you through a lengthy and very detailed dissection of a complicated play in its attempt to demonstrate how using dramatic questions can help keep your play active and suspenseful. The rule to keep in mind is that there should never be a moment in your play in which there is no question in the air. Every single line should either:

1. raise a question,
2. help somehow delay the answer to that question, or
3. provide an answer to that question.

Wherever possible, those lines or moments that fall into category 2 might well be lines that actually raise or answer another question. Review the first act of *Othello* again and notice how interwoven the qp's are. Notice that Shakespeare keeps returning time and again to the very first question raised: Will Iago get Roderigo to calm down? He finally does, in act 4. What happens?

Keep in mind how dramatic questions form the bases for your assorted miniplays, and be sure, again, that there is always some sort of negotiation (i.e., *not* just conversation) going on between two people.

Exercise 8:2

Write an eight-line scene as follows:

LINE 1	Raise a QI
LINE 2	Answer QI, raise another QI
LINE 3	Answer second QI, raise a qp
LINE 4	
LINE 5	
LINE 6	
LINE 7	Answer qp. Raise another qp.
LINE 8	Raise another question of any sort.

Exercise 8:3

Here is a short scene between Bill and Mary. It's deliberately written to be static and dull. Your job: rewrite it so that the very first line raises a qp that is not answered until the end. Add whatever you need to the situation. Just keep it suspenseful.

> BILL: It's five o'clock.
> MARY: It's pretty early.
> BILL: Not too early I hope.
> MARY: It's always early at five o'clock.
> BILL: That's your opinion.
> MARY: Who else's do I have to go by?
> BILL: I think it's right on the button.
> MARY: You would.
> BILL: After all . . .

It's now in your hands. Make it work.

Revision Questions

There are any number of responses to your early work that can clue you in to how boring, static, dull, or uninteresting your play is—or at least sections of it. Often people will find exposition heavy, flat, and obvious. Or they will note that your characters spend too much time discussing things, or engaging in what's often called psychobabble, which is having one character tell another what's wrong with him or her or describing an emotional state. Any number of such responses should encourage you to ask these questions:

1. If you examine your play, moment by moment as you did in the last chapter, can you locate those moments in which no question is raised or current? How can you rewrite the moment in order to raise a question? Can you make us curious about information?

2. Have you made sure that a question of plot is in the air of your play at every single moment? When one is ended, how soon do you begin another? Unless it's "immediately," it may not be soon enough.

3. Sometimes a way to fix a small scene is to begin it with a qp—as small as it is—to keep things going. Can you make the beginning of each miniplay a line that raises a qp?

Part Three

Some Advanced Tricks

9

The Pigeon Sister

I need to begin this chapter with a nod to Neil Simon. It was while teaching his play *The Odd Couple* that I was able to crystallize this concept, and thus its name is both an indication of what it is and an acknowledgment of its source.

Let me describe the play to you if you don't know it, or refresh your memory if you do. Both Felix and Oscar are divorced men, who in the course of the first act, decide to live together. One of them is a freewheeling, easy-going slob who takes life as it is. That's Oscar. The other, Felix, is the complete opposite: anal-retentive, compulsively neat, and a bit of a hypochondriac. Their two personalities are just destined to crash eventually.

Let's examine the structure Simon has created. The first act sets up the situation in a series of well-constructed miniplays. A quick rundown reveals some of them are about:

- how the card game should be played;
- Oscar doing something about the missing Felix;
- Oscar keeping Felix from killing himself;
- Oscar convincing Felix to move in with him.

At the end of act 1, Felix does move in.

Act 2 continues with more miniplays showing us how the relationship between Oscar and Felix has changed and are about:

- the new kind of poker game that's going on;
- Oscar threatening to do something drastic.

And then the play runs out of steam. We've seen the two men together; we know how their lives have changed; we've had perhaps too many variations on the same old gag involving the nice guy and the slob. By the time we get to the middle of the first scene of act 2, Simon is clearly running out of plot, not to mention jokes. He needs something new to kick the play into a higher gear with new action. And it's precisely at this point that Simon has Oscar say, "Like unless I get to touch something soft in the next two weeks, I'm in big trouble." And the play is off and running in a clear, new, and interesting direction. Turns out that two young ladies have moved in upstairs: Cecily and Gwendolyn Pigeon. Oscar has his eye on them, and of course, is referring to the possibility of sex with them when he talks about "touch[ing] something soft." The rest of the play is now about whether or not Oscar will get Felix to help him score with the women. And driving toward this goal there follows a whole series of miniplays about:

- the lateness of dinner;
- whether Felix will go through with the plans;
- getting acquainted with the girls;
- fixing drinks;
- Felix sharing his family miseries with the girls;
- Oscar trying to save the evening;
- what happens the next day; and
- how Oscar and Felix have both been changed by this experience.

In other words, the introduction of this new plot twist has been nothing more than a device to generate new action. And it's this device that forms the subject of this chapter; a device that—for want of a better word—I've named the *Pigeon Sister*.

A Pigeon Sister is any device or event or situation that arises in the play over which two or more characters can interact. It's both a catalyst and a focus, engaging these characters in activities—it is something that makes them have to *do* things. It's sometimes called the *story hook*, the peg on which to hang the action to follow. Most important, think of it as that device that turns a situation into a drama.

Examine every any sitcom you've ever watched. Every episode uses virtually the same characters with the same personality quirks involved in the same relationships. The situation never changes. What does perpetually change, however, is the Pigeon Sister: Every week some new catalyst or event gives all the characters something different to do. Sometimes it's a new person who comes into the mix. Sometimes it's a problem one character is having at work. Sometimes it's a surprise. Sometimes it's not. If you ever watched the TV version of the *Odd Couple,* you've seen this at work. Felix has trouble with his job. Oscar needs money for a present. Felix loses an object of importance. Oscar has to attend a sport event on an important night for Felix. The wives often appear. Other relatives appear. One of them has a cold. On and on and on, for seven seasons.

What's important to understand is that a Pigeon Sister makes people *do* things, not just *talk* about them. In *The Odd Couple,* it leads to a wide variety of actions: preparing dinner, setting up the right atmosphere, trying to make conversation, looking at photos, sharing sob stories, fighting over what to do about the rest of the evening, and so forth. Pigeon Sisters are intimately related to miniplays: in a sense, every miniplay might contain its own Pigeon Sister.

Furthermore, you'll note that a Pigeon Sister might contain within it another, smaller Pigeon Sister, which serves the same function as a miniplay within a miniplay. If you examine the first part of act 2, scene 2, you'll note that Felix and Oscar are at odds over the dinner that Felix has prepared. Oscar comes home later than planned, and the food is ruined. They quarrel over it. Felix tries to save it, and so forth. There is one moment when Oscar and Felix argue over what the dinner is: Oscar calls it spaghetti, and Felix tells him it's linguini. Oscar then picks up a handful and throws it against the kitchen wall, declaring, "Now it's garbage." Dealing with the linguini is a Pigeon Sister for:

- quarreling over the spoiled dinner, which is a Pigeon Sister for
- Oscar and Felix at odds again, which is a Pigeon Sister for
- fixing dinner for the two ladies, which is a Pigeon Sister for
- seducing the two ladies, which is a Pigeon Sister for

- the whole line of action about the Pigeon Sisters, which itself is a Pigeon Sister for
- the entire second half of the play, which itself is a Pigeon Sister for the whole play.

Sounds a little complicated, but it's really not. It goes back to questions of plot, which we discussed in the last chapter. It also goes back to the issue of complications and strategies that we looked in chapters 4 and 5: a Pigeon Sister is a crisis, an obstacle, and an IN ORDER TO, all working together. Your characters must always be *doing* something and not just talking. Each little Pigeon Sister gives them something to *do*.

A Pigeon Sister Is Not an Argument

Before we move on, it's very important that you understand the difference between this device and what is really only an argument. It's easy to confuse the two, but one is dramatic and interesting while the other is just talk. Here's an example that might help clarify the difference.

Let's say you have two characters like Oscar and Felix; we'll call them Sam and Charlie. You want to let us see that one is paranoid, while the other is free and easy. The issue right now is beer. They're out of it. It's a situation. The scene might go like this:

SAM: I need you to get me some beer.

CHARLIE: I'm watching my show.

SAM: You never do what I ask.

CHARLIE: You always interrupt my programs.

SAM: Remember, I pay two thirds of the rent here.

CHARLIE: Yeah, which is usually three days late. I do the dishes.

SAM: You're such a jerk.

CHARLIE: You had lousy toilet training. Did anybody ever tell you that?

And on and on. The two men are sitting in their chairs quarreling. The quarrel may range over many topics and give us some insights into each personality, but it's essentially a static scene. It's what we often call psychobabble; a passage of dialogue in which characters describe someone else's—or often their own—personality. It's not active, and it's deadly boring. Let's create a useful Pigeon Sister for them.

SAM: You seen my car keys?

CHARLIE: Did you look in your pants?

SAM: Why would they be in my pants? They're more likely to be in YOUR pants.

CHARLIE: Very funny. I'm watching the game.

SAM: We're out of beer. I need to get to Willy's before they close.

CHARLIE: Take my car.

SAM: You know I can't drive a stick. Maybe they're in the sofa. Let me see.

CHARLIE: They're not in the sofa.

SAM: Come on, get up.

CHARLIE: (reluctantly climbs out of the sofa. Sam starts upending the cushions.) You do this all the time.

SAM: Look underneath, will ya?

CHARLIE: (starting to leave the room) I'm not crawling on my knees. I'm getting your pants.

SAM: Take one step and I'll fling this beer at you.

CHARLIE: Last time you lost your keys we uprooted the whole house and we wound up finding them in your cuffs.

SAM: That was New Year's Eve. New Year's Eve doesn't count.

CHARLIE: I'll bet you ten bucks that's where they are.

SAM: You stay out of my pants.

CHARLIE: You put down that glass.

And so on.

Do you see the difference? In the first scene, the only thing they do is talk to each other. We learn how different they are only because they describe each other's quirks. In the second, they get busy doing things: getting up, looking under the sofa, starting to go for Sam's pants, and so forth. We learn how different they are by the kinds of things they choose to do or not to do. The Pigeon Sister has been the car keys. At one point, the pants become the Pigeon Sister for the car keys; and at another point, the sofa cushions have become another Pigeon Sister for the car keys. And the car keys itself would most likely have been a Pigeon Sister for getting the beer, while getting the beer is surely some larger Pigeon Sister for the whole play—whatever that might be.

In fact, if you like, you can go over the second scene and notice that there are several key dramatic questions running through it:

QI: Has Charlie seen the keys?
qp: Will Sam get Charlie to respond?
qp: Will Sam find his keys?
qp: Will Sam get Charlie to help him look; i.e., get off the couch?
qp: Will Charlie get Sam to look in his pants?
qp: Will Sam keep Charlie away from his pants?
qp: Will Charlie keep Sam from flinging the beer at him?

Another Extended Example

A Pigeon Sister provides a vehicle for action. It turns conversations into negotiations. It turns differences into conflicts. It provides the "thing" for miniplays to be about. It creates opportunities for your characters to "do something" rather than simply "talk about something."

Let's look at another example to help clarify this. Since we've spent so much time earlier on *Othello*, let's turn our attention instead to *The Glass Menagerie*. This is a useful play to examine because many people find the play extremely dull and talky. Granted the talk may be poetic and the characters intriguing, but as a play, it definitely lacks action. Let me try to demonstrate the difference between conversation and a Pigeon Sister by taking you through some of its scenes.

Look at the very opening scene, following the narration. Amanda's second speech involves a Pigeon Sister: the issue of saying grace. While there *is* no activity about it, there could be. For example: Tom could insist it is Laura's turn; Laura could look for her book of daily meditations; and so on.

As soon as Tom sits down at the table, a Pigeon Sister about how to eat occupies the characters. When Tom has had enough of his mother's badgering, there is a brief Pigeon Sister concerning smoking. Then there's another brief one about bringing in the wine, followed by mention of "gentlemen callers." At first glance, you might think that these male visitors become the next working Pigeon Sister, but they don't. They are not vehicles for action, but rather a subject for a long series of monologues about them. Amanda talks, Tom and Laura listen. But the three don't engage themselves in doing anything about them.

Could this miniplay be more dramatic? Could a Pigeon Sister be derived from the issue of gentlemen callers? Yes, of course, by providing something each of the characters could *do* or *not do* about them. Perhaps Tom wants his mother to stop talking about them and asks her for more potatoes. However, Laura wants to hear more and urges Amanda to tell another story. The Pigeon Sister would be Amanda's decision about telling or not telling another story. Or suppose there were a phone number in the play—Amanda remembers an old chum who might have a son Laura's age, and the three have to decide whether or not Amanda makes that call.

But Tennessee Williams doesn't go that route. He lets the matter just be conversation. You can tell there's no Pigeon Sister because there is no *question of plot* in the air. However, a few scenes later down the road, we will see exactly how Mr. Williams *does* create a Pigeon Sister out of the gentleman caller; he makes it the central core of the entire play.

In the meantime, when does he involve the *next* Pigeon Sister? When Laura suggests that she will clear the table? Possibly. If Amanda and Tom were to offer to help Laura; or if Laura started and then had trouble and needed help; or if all three were in any active way involved in the decision or process of clearing the table. But Amanda gets up to do it, and the matter is quickly over.

No, there hasn't been any major or significant Pigeon Sister so far, although there were some interesting possibilities. Now turn to scene 2, in which a similar problem exists: Nearly all of the scene is Amanda's struggle to get the truth out of Laura. She asks; Laura answers. The subject of the conversation changes, but it is still conversation. There is a small moment when a Pigeon Sister does appear—when Laura fetches the high school yearbook and shares some memories about the boy in the choir. It doesn't amount to much, but it does give the two women something to do together. And another small one almost appears—when Laura goes over to the phonograph to start playing it. Amanda could protest that now is not the time (something she actually does in the final moments of the play), but again Williams chooses not to create something larger. This is one reason many people find the first part of this play very dull and hard to sit through. While lots of things are being said, nothing is being *done* on either a small scale or a large one.

What happens in scene 3? We first hear some more narration from Tom, in which the major dramatic question of plot is raised. When he tells us "the idea of getting a gentleman caller for Laura began to play a more and more important part in Mother's calculations," we know where the play is going, and we have the four keys in hand. The Pigeon Sister of the play has been established: The Gentleman Caller. From here on out, as in *The Odd Couple,* all the characters' actions are centered on this one catalyst.

Hopefully, the concept is becoming clear, and you're beginning to understand the difference between discussion and drama. One more scene ought to do it; the hardest scene of all. Skip ahead to scene 7. The four are at the dinner table, when suddenly the lights go out. What to do about the lights becomes a Pigeon Sister. Then this little Pigeon Sister itself has one: dealing with the candles and maneuvering in the dark. You may have noticed that the electric bill that Tom hasn't paid could have been a Pigeon Sister, but it's not. It's just a bit of exposition tossed in. Actually, it's an *obstacle* that interrupts the dinner party.

Amanda uses Tom's "carelessness" as an excuse to make him join her washing dishes, leaving Laura alone with Jim and suggesting he bring her a small glass of wine. Thus, washing the dirty dishes has become a small Pigeon Sister, as has the glass of wine.

As Amanda and Tom move offstage, Jim goes to visit Laura. Their conversation now runs about fifteen minutes of stage time. It's essentially just two strangers getting to know each other, a situation fraught with pitfalls for a dramatist. How to keep the scene lively? How to engage the characters in action rather than just dull conversation? Let's track what Williams does.

Jim offers her wine, which she accepts. The wine is a very small Pigeon Sister. Jim wonders where to set the candle, leading to another small Pigeon Sister: sitting down and getting comfortable. Once "getting comfortable" is over, Jim offers her a stick of chewing gum, a potential Pigeon Sister that never gets going. (What can you think of to do with that gum?)

Now we have talk. Jim talks about the world's fair; Laura inquires about his singing; they share memories of high school; Jim remembers "Blue Roses," and there's an extended sequence of revelations about themselves. It's very pretty, but essentially static and potentially dull. If anything keeps the scene alive, it is a series of questions of information.

Laura gets up to show Jim her high school yearbook, and they look through it. There's a small Pigeon Sister involving signing the yearbook. It doesn't go very far, although it could have. (How? What could you invent to expand this little yearbook into a major Pigeon Sister? Jim can't find a pen; Laura gets up to get one from a drawer, Jim tries to help her; she is reluctant to accept his help; he convinces her it'll be like a game, etc.)

Laura then asks about Emily Meisenbach, Jim's girlfriend. This leads into a question-and-answer sequence, "What have you done since high school?" which involves shared memories again. Laura mentions her glass menagerie, but Jim doesn't pick up on it. Instead, Jim goes into a long sequence of psychobabble, describing what's wrong with Laura and what's right about himself.

There's more conversation, until—what? Can you spot the next Pigeon Sister of any note? Laura picks up the glass unicorn, and they talk about the glass menagerie. Is this a Pigeon Sister? No; it's just another subject for conversation. Could it have been a Pigeon Sister? Well, as we'll see, it becomes a very important one a few minutes later.

But no, the very next useful Pigeon Sister that arises is when Jim asks Laura to dance. An important moment indeed, it gets both of them *doing* something together. And, of course, that leads into the next useful Pigeon Sister: when Jim breaks the glass animal.

But then, once the issue of the broken toy is over, the scene resumes its psychobabble, as Jim tries to make Laura feel better.

There's a lovely little Pigeon Sister in Jim's clumsy attempt to kiss Laura and make her feel better, followed by a very tiny one about the Life Saver candy.

This is followed by Jim's revelation of his fiancée, Betty. This is an important obstacle, but it is not a Pigeon Sister. It does give rise, however, to a very important question of character: What will this information do to Laura?

Her heart broken, Laura then introduces another small Pigeon Sister. Can you spot it? Yes: it's the glass animal again.

And right after that, bam: in come Amanda and Tom to interrupt. The play quickly comes to its conclusion. The rest of the scene consists of:

- a Pigeon Sister about lemonade;
- a conversation about leaving;
- a conversation revealing the news of Jim's engagement to Betty;
- a Pigeon Sister about Jim's leaving;
- a Pigeon Sister about the victrola;
- a Pigeon Sister about Tom's going to the movies;

And then Tom leaves, only to appear at the side and deliver his final speech, which is a final Pigeon Sister about traveling.

Thus, the whole scene uses a clever mix of memories interrupted by occasional Pigeon Sisters. It has moments of onstage action interwoven with passages of psychobabble and shared revelations. It is two-thirds static and only partially active. It's important that you see where these different techniques are used.

A small digression, because this almost always comes up in my classes. "Well," somebody asks, "if it's two-thirds static, why is it so interesting on stage?" The answer is because of the urgency of the question of plot that lies underneath it. Remember, the overall question is, "Will Amanda find a husband for Laura?" We've seen how desperate this search is, how important it is for Amanda, how much effort she's put into making it happen. The scene between Jim and Laura is the climax and final answer to that question. We in the audience have been expecting this scene for over an hour. It's this anticipation that keeps it going for us and lets us sit through the psychobabble, waiting for the answer.

Exercise 9:1

Help Tennessee Williams improve his play. Suggest five different Pigeon Sisters he might have created for this scene we've just analyzed. What other activities might the two engage in that would help reveal character without so much psychobabble and discussion? I've included a list below. You invent others.

- There are some pieces of candy left.
- Jim remembers a song from the opera and invites Laura to sing with him.
- Jim looks at his watch to see the time and sees it has run down.
- The candle burns out, dripping wax on the floor.

What can you come up with?

Revision Questions

The Pigeon Sisters can be extremely useful devices to help keep your scenes lively and active. If you choose them carefully, they can also reveal character—in the same way that choosing obstacles and strategies can.

You may have noticed, as we've trucked through *The Glass Menagerie,* that I've continually made references to the material in two previous chapters: miniplays and dramatic questions. The Pigeon Sister, as you've seen, is very closely related to the miniplay and the dramatic question. Since all miniplays have questions of plot, and all questions of plot involve immediate activity, the Pigeon Sister becomes what the activity revolves around and often involves goals, obstacles, and strategies itself. When your audience loses attention or complains there's not enough action, revisit every moment to see whether the problem lies with the Pigeon Sisters.

1. Is the scene active, or merely conversation? While the scene may appear to you to move along, is it simply because your characters have changed the topic of conversation?

2. Where do you find moments of psychobabble, wherein characters describe each other's personalities?

3. What Pigeon Sisters can you invent that will get the characters actively engaged in doing something?

4. How can these Pigeon Sisters show different sides of each character's personality?

5. Overall, where can you invent Pigeon Sisters, clarify questions of plot, create miniplays? These are all tools to help you enliven the static and dull parts of your play.

10

The Exposition Pig

Every writer of realistic plays comes up against this problem sooner or later: How on earth do you reveal to the audience the information they need in order to understand what's going on? Where does the action take place? Who are these people; what are their names; and what are they doing in this room? What happened in the past that makes everybody so upset? What time is it, if it matters? What actually happened at the dance that night that made Laverne commit suicide? Who is that other person that just came in? You'll note, of course, that all of these are *questions of information*; and since you are well versed in writing miniplays that use QI's, you now need to find ways in which to answer them. I use the term *exposition pig* when this is done badly, because the fact that you are stopping the action in order to give us this information sticks out like a big fat pig waddling through the room. I'm in debt to several of my playwriting students for the name.

What are some solutions to the problem of bad exposition? Actually, there are two problems to deal with. (1) What does the audience actually need to know? And (2) how can you get it into the play gracefully?

How Much Do You Need to Know?

A problem often faced by beginning writers or early drafts is to decide exactly how much—and exactly what—does the audience really need to know? And in most cases, it's surprisingly little.

Remember that plays never take place in the past; they always take place in the present, looking toward the future. Therefore, the only information we need to know is that which makes a difference to the future. Examine some famous realistic plays and note just how little you actually do know.

In *The Glass Menagerie,* what offstage events are important enough to be onstage? All that we know about Amanda's marriage is that she married a "telephone man who fell in love with long distance" and abandoned them. We know nothing about the kind of marriage they had, how the children were raised, or exactly what event caused him to leave. All that we know about Laura's mishap in business school is that she threw up and stopped going. All that we know about Amanda's childhood is that she had lots of gentlemen callers and collected jonquils one summer. We don't know a whole lot—because nothing else is important.

Similarly, in *Othello,* we know very little about the past:

- somehow Cassio got promoted before Iago;
- somehow Iago made a deal with Roderigo about Desdemona;
- somehow Othello was able to woo and win Desdemona;
- for some reason, Cassio can't hold his liquor;
- at some time in the past, Cassio fooled around with a woman named Bianca;
- at some point in the past, Othello gave Desdemona a handkerchief.

What do we *not* know? We know nothing about how Othello got to be a general; why and how he came to trust Iago; why he promoted Cassio first; what kind of childhood Othello had; why he would marry outside his race; why the Duke trusts him so. We know that later Othello gets called back to Venice, but we never know exactly why. We have no clue about the kind of soldier Iago was; why he lost the promotion; how he met and married Emilia; why Emilia puts up with him; how Cassio met Bianca; what happened in the battle that Othello seems to have won; and so forth.

In short, both Williams and Shakespeare give us just enough to understand what's going on, and no more. Of course, there are other plays in which we get a great deal of the past. In *A Doll's House,* for instance, we need to know all of the details of Nora's marriage to Torvald; exactly what Torvald does for a living; precisely what it was Nora did that makes her susceptible to blackmail; who the various men in her life are and where they come from; and what sort of friendship Mrs. Linde has with Nora. This is because Ibsen, in this play, is dealing with the traps that society lays for us. He is trying to show the evil effects of the laws that have put Nora in her desperate position; he is trying to contrast Nora's poor upbringing with Mrs. Linde's success at surviving; he is trying to paint Torvald as a man who subscribes to the false values his position demands of him; and so forth.

In Eugene O'Neill's later plays, *Long Day's Journey into Night, A Moon for the Misbegotten,* and *The Iceman Cometh,* whole acts are given over to one character telling another about his or her past—but that's because, like Ibsen, O'Neill is showing characters trapped by their past lives and unable to break themselves out of it. Each character has memories that are haunting him or her, making their present lives and actions miserable.

How Does Knowing about the Past Affect the Future?

In general, information about the past typically affects the future in several key ways.

It's Going to Change the Future

Many realistic plays are about characters who are desperately trying to change their lives. When this is the case, we need to know what situation they are escaping. In these plays, the past becomes a motive for the present action. Some examples: In *A Streetcar Named Desire,* Blanche has come to New Orleans to make a fresh start in her life. In *Death of a Salesman,* both Willy and Biff are planning a big meeting tomorrow: Biff wants a job, Willy wants a career move. In *The Cherry Orchard,* Lopakhin tries to convince the family to sell the orchard and break out of their poverty. In *Who's Afraid of Virginia Woolf,* all four characters are seeking, like O'Neill's characters, a way of redeeming their past mistakes.

It's Going to Contrast with the Future

Other plays are about characters who are trying to achieve something immediate or more limited. In these plays, characters are often accidentally changed by their journey. They learn something, take on different personalities, make new decisions, or are changed in other ways. They've accidentally become new people. In these cases, it's important for us to get a glimpse of the people they were before.

In *Speed-the-Plow,* Bobby realizes he's been duped by this strange girl and comes to a new understanding of his role in the film industry. What's important to know is how he perceived himself before this encounter. We see him joking and baiting Charlie before the mysterious girl shows up.

In *Our Town,* Emily realizes—when she visits her twelfth birthday—how important every day of our lives is. Before that, she had her mind on more superficial things and never thought about "clocks ticking and new iron-dresses." In the first two acts, we see her being childish and immature before she dies.

In *Romeo and Juliet,* both kids change from being headstrong young puppies in heat to becoming mature, self-sacrificing tragic heroes. We see Romeo pining for his old girlfriend before he falls in love with Juliet.

How Do You Get the Facts into the Play?

Once you've determined what about the past is necessary to reveal, your challenge becomes finding graceful ways of bringing it into the play. In other words, how do you avoid an intrusion by the Exposition Pig? Here are some suggestions.

Use Presentational Devices

The easiest way to tell the audience about the past is simply to have a character step forward and make a speech; this is often done in presentational plays, in which the fourth wall—that imaginary divide between the audience and what happens onstage—is broken. Euripides does this, for instance, at the opening of *Hippolytus,* wherein he has the goddess Aphrodite step forward and tell us what the current marital situation of Hippolytus and Phaedra is. In *Our Town,* Thornton Wilder uses the Stage Manager constantly to tell the audience who's who, what's what, and where's where. You'll find a presentation device in the opening narrations in *Romeo and Juliet, Henry V,* and *Richard III,* as well as in recent plays by Donald Marguiles, Neil LaBute, Richard Greenberg, and others. It's a simple and easy device that can save you a great deal of time and energy, as long as it's appropriate to the style of your play.

Most plays, however, try not to break that fourth wall and thus pose the problem of making people talk about the past in a somewhat realistic fashion. In these cases, I have found that one overall rule generally works.

Use the Past

Now is a good time to review the material in chapter 5 on strategies and in chapter 7 on the miniplay. In both, we discussed how revealing information can be active: when one character uses facts about the past as a tool or a weapon. People typically only reveal facts about the past because they want to achieve something in the moment. Consider in your situation what the miniplay is about and how one character is trying to get something from another, using information strategically.

In the case of *Othello,* notice the moments in which Iago reveals what's going on to Roderigo because he's trying to calm him down. Notice how Iago reveals to Brabantio what's happened because he wants to rile him up and cause havoc. Notice how Brabantio brings his case to the Duke and how Othello answers the Duke's questions because they each want the Duke to judge in their favor. Notice that each fact brought into the play is used by one character as a strategy against another.

How do people use the past?

People need information because they want to make a decision. Thus, in act 1, scene 2 of *The Glass Menagerie,* Amanda questions Laura all about her experiences in the business school, all about her high school crush, and all about her dreams and hopes—because she needs to decide what to do about Laura's future.

People reveal facts because they want somebody else to make a decision. In *The Cherry Orchard,* Lopakhin time and time again brings up the problem of the cherry orchard, reminding his family of the crisis, because he wants them to take action.. The girl in *Speed-the-Plow* brings up Bobby's past to him because she wants him to approve the movie she wants to make. Nearly all the facts that are disclosed in the first act of *Othello* are, as we've seen, of this type.

People reveal facts because they want to teach or inform somebody else about something that is important. In *Miss Julie,* Christine tells Jean all about Miss Julie's bad behavior because essentially she wants to warn him to stay away. In *A Doll's House,* Mrs. Linde reveals her life story to Nora because she's trying to show Nora another way of life. In *The Glass Menagerie,* Amanda tells the long story about her jonquils because she's trying to get Laura and Tom to understand her life and perhaps change their opinions of her seemingly foolish behavior.

People reveal facts because they want forgiveness or understanding from somebody else, or to somehow become closer to or bond with another. Have you noticed in your life how often you will share confidences with a stranger that you wouldn't share with your closest friend? Is it because deep inside we all need to confess or unburden ourselves? In *A Streetcar Named Desire,* Blanche tells Mitch all about the death of her first husband because she wants him to fall in love with her. In *A Moon for the Misbegotten,* Jamie tells Josie all about the tragic train ride when he got drunk, because he wants to unburden himself and find forgiveness.

People reveal facts because they want to hurt or destroy somebody. In *A Long Day's Journey into Night,* almost every fact that is brought into the open is used by one character to wound, humiliate, or attack somebody else. Edmund's birth, Tyrone's stinginess, Mary's addiction, and Jamie's alcoholism—time and time again, the past becomes a weapon.

People reveal facts because they want to achieve any number of things from somebody else. Never put a fact into the play without somehow involving it in a miniplay, in which one character uses it as a strategy.

Don't Tell Us: Show Us

This course is always the most useful of all. If you can, find a way to actually let us see what happens or has happened that's so important. Ever since Elmer Rice introduced the flashback, in his 1920 play *Counsellor at Law,* this device has become more and more prevalent in realistic dramas. Writers play free and easy with time and often take us directly into the past as a sort of side trip on our journey into the future. In *Sight Unseen,* for instance, Donald Margulies intersperses three different timelines: One level is what is happening here tonight; a second shows us scenes in the past lives of the painter and his ex-girlfriend; and a third shows us several different parts of an interview the painter has had with a probing talk-show host. In *Proof,* David Auburn suddenly, in the middle of act 2, takes us back several years for a fifteen-minute scene. Audiences are used to these sudden time-shifts, and they are often the most effective way of letting us see and understand the past. In *How I Learned to Drive,* Paula Vogel mixes the past and present constantly, using a narrator and written scene titles projected on a screen to show us exactly what happened that brought us to where we are now.

As an alternative to the flashback, consider beginning the play at an earlier point in time, so that we actually see the past move into the present. There's nothing to prevent your setting the first scene at Jill's tenth birthday party and gradually moving forward. O'Neill does this constantly; of course, his plays are hours long, but they are powerful in their own way.

Exercise 10:1

Consider the following facts:

- Steve is twenty-five years old, and today is his birthday.
- When he was ten, he stole a watch from his father's friend.
- Steve is applying for a job as a bank teller.
- His sister is getting married in three months.
- Steve used to be a boy scout.

Create a short play in which you somehow manage to bring all these facts into the present action. You can invent whatever characters you need and use as many different devices as you wish.

Revision Question

Examine your play closely and make a list of all the facts you have brought into the play. Examine your list to determine which of these facts are absolutely necessary and which are only extensions or elaborations. Eliminate all facts but those which you feel are needed in order for the play to make sense. Examine the scenes in which these facts appear and see how you can make miniplays out of these moments.

11

Miscellaneous Tricks

This chapter is a catch-all for a number of useful tricks that often help in early drafts of a play. Sometimes you can play with these first, to help you generate ideas, but they are more helpful when you're working on revisions. Applying one or more of them to your play or idea can often shed light on how to solve trouble spots. I call them the four "T's":

- the Torvald moment
- triangles
- why today?
- the turnabout

The Torvald Moment

First of all, who is Torvald? Any student of theater will, at some point, read Ibsen's masterpiece, *A Doll's House*. The play concerns the problem facing a young woman named Nora, married to a man named Torvald. Nora is being blackmailed by a man named Krogstad. It seems that years ago, Nora forged her father's signature on a loan application; she needed money to take her ailing husband abroad. Torvald is ignorant of all this for most of the play. Only at the end does he find out what Nora has done. He is furious. He accuses her of being a useless wife, a dangerous mother, a liar, and a very bad person. His position, his financial security, his very reputation are suddenly on the line.

However, at the very moment Torvald is berating her, a letter arrives from Krogstad. For reasons too complicated to go into here, Krogstad has changed his mind and removed his threat. Nora is in the clear. When he reads this letter, Torvald calls out: "Nora, my darling; do you see what this means. I am saved, Nora; I am saved!"

To which Nora replies, quietly but with deadly effect: "And what of me?"

This brings Torvald to his senses, and he excuses himself: "Of course you. Both of us." But it's too late. In that one unguarded moment, when his defenses were down and he had no time to think or prevaricate, Torvald has spontaneously uttered words of naked truth that suddenly show us deep inside his personality. All of his pretensions, his selfishness, his fears for his reputation—all these secrets are revealed by that one explosive line.

Many plays have similar moments. I've labeled this device the *Torvald moment*, in homage to Ibsen and his genius. It should be obvious that plays that have such moments are meant to be psychologically realistic. The moment usually comes as the climax of a scene of high emotion and great tension, often in the heat of an argument.

Here are some examples. In Edward Albee's *Who's Afraid of Virginia Woolf,* George and Martha are arguing, once again. Martha has the upper hand, as she always does. Their marriage is rotten, built upon lies and self-deceptions. George has bitterly blamed Martha for their unhappiness. At one point in an ongoing argument, George wants to call it quits; he cries out, "I cannot stand it!" And Martha shoots back: "You can stand it!! You married me for it!" With her words clearly exposing George's weakness and self-deception, he sees the naked truth about himself.

In the musical *Gypsy,* Gypsy Rose Lee—whose real name is Louise—is quarreling with her mother, Rose. Rose claims she has sacrificed her own career for Louise's and now accuses Louise of trying to dump her, claiming that success had made Louise ungrateful. Each brings up, in psychobabble, issues from the past. As Rose heatedly attacks her daughter, at one point she cries out, "All those years, who was I doing it for?" To which Louise replies, cool and calm, "I thought you did it for me, Momma," reflecting back to Rose her selfish craving for the success she never had.

In David Mamet's *Speed-the-Plow,* Bobby and Charlie are quarreling. Bobby has promised to work with Charlie on getting the green light for a movie. Bobby has just told Charlie that he's changed his mind: he's going to work with this young woman who has made him think about doing good in the world, rather than making commercially successful but garbage films. Charlie is trying to get Bobby to realize that the woman is a fake who only pretended to be virtuous in order to get her first climb up the ladder of Hollywood success. Time is running out: Bobby has to report to his boss within minutes, giving Charlie only seconds in which to expose her for the fraud he is convinced she is. He attacks her, he confuses Bobby, he stalls and railroads her attempts to prove her innocence, until in a fit of frustrated anger and desperation, the woman cries out, "Bobby, we have a meeting!"

What is going on? Well, earlier we've learned that "having meetings" is the most important part of climbing the ladder of Hollywood success. When Bobby now hears the young woman speaking career-obsessive language, he suddenly sees her for what she really is. There is a pause. Charlie says, "I rest my case." The woman asks, "What happened?," failing to realize how she has exposed herself.

Do you see the pattern? In each instance, the fateful Torvald moment has come at the peak of a scene of great emotional confrontation in which the characters have little or no time to be rational. Their emotions get the best of them. Of course, in each instance, the early parts of the play have provided us with enough information to truly appreciate the revealed truth. We've seen George and Martha going at each other; we've seen Rose manipulate and coerce her children; we've seen Bobby and Charlie plan around this important meeting and learned their Hollywood lingo.

Exercise 11:1

Look for such a moment in *Othello;* do you find one? If not, how would you write one? Perhaps, in some quarrel with Othello, Iago accidentally says, "You should have given that promotion to me!" Suddenly his secret motive has been revealed, and Othello might now see what a jealous monster he's created. Or perhaps in a similar heated moment (when Iago is with Cassio), Iago accidentally boasts about the power he has over women, how he's even gotten his own wife to steal from Desdemona. Suddenly a clue about the missing handkerchief is uncovered. What could happen in a scene between Iago and Roderigo to cause Roderigo to suddenly see the light?

How Can You Use the Torvald Moment?

First, you need to decide if your play warrants such a moment. Is your work largely character-driven or not? Do the subtle complexities of people's personalities make much difference to the outcome or not? Would such a moment be effective at the climax?

If so, the second step is to decide what that line would be. What sentence, what insight, what outcry would your character *most want* to keep hidden? Perhaps it's something about himself that he doesn't know—perhaps there's a self-revelation that, given its intensity, would destroy the lies and illusions he's created. What would the speech, line, or phrase be?

Third, set up a scene of intense emotional confrontation that would provide fertile soil for the line to emerge. What would your character be quarreling about? And with whom? What information must we have in advance to fully appreciate the importance of the line? What will happen immediately after the line has been uttered?

How can you create such a scene? If you remember our work on strategies, you'll recall that working backwards and drafting an "in-order-to" chart can often help you arrange your scenes. If you place this Torvald moment at the top of your chart and work backwards from it, you'll likely find the structure you need to make the moment effective.

Triangles

As a device, the *triangle* is closely related to the Pigeon Sister. If Sam and Charlie (or Oscar and Felix, for that matter) are engaged in conflicting actions involving somebody or something else, that person or thing forms the third point of a triangle. If the third point is inanimate, such as the car keys, you have an interesting drama in which we can see how each of the other two behave.

However, if the third part of the triangle is *another character,* you have great potential for a complex pattern of shifting relationships, power struggles, interactions, and conflicts. If A and B are fighting over C, what happens if A and C join against B; or if B and C join against A? What other variations can you play upon these possible combinations?

In *Othello,* Shakespeare has richly created a plethora of triangles. Each has its own little play; each suggests appropriate goals and obstacles and strategies; each provides opportunities for miniplays. In each case, one of the three sides works as a Pigeon Sister for the other two, and so on. Here are some that come to mind:

> Iago, Roderigo, and Desdemona: Notice how Iago keeps holding out Desdemona as bait for Roderigo.
>
> Iago, Cassio, and Desdemona: Notice how Iago uses their friendship; how Cassio depends upon each of the other two for his plan to work; how Desdemona agrees with Iago's plan and Cassio's request. Notice there are scenes throughout the play in which two of these characters are talking about or negotiating over the third, such as when Iago convinces Cassio to get help from Desdemona.
>
> Cassio, Othello, and Desdemona: Notice how Cassio tries to use Desdemona to help him with Othello; how Desdemona tries to influence Othello to forgive Cassio; how Othello becomes insanely jealous in his suspicions about them.
>
> Iago, Desdemona, and Emilia: Notice how Iago uses Emilia to help him get to Desdemona (in regard to the handkerchief); how Desdemona relies on Emilia to help understand Iago; how Emilia is torn between her twin duties; and how she behaves at the end.

Smaller triangles include:

> Brabantio, Iago, and Roderigo
> Brabantio, Othello, and the Duke

Brabantio, Othello, and Desdemona
Cassio, Iago, and Bianca
Iago, Cassio, and Roderigo
Desdemona, Othello, and Emilia
Othello, Iago, and the representatives from Venice (Lodovico)

Each of these triangles becomes the material for a plot development, a scene, or a miniplay: One uses another as an ally against the third; one uses another as a strategy against the third; one uses another as an obstacle in relation to the third; one becomes a Pigeon Sister in an interaction with the third. Each possible permutation provides material for a powerful scene.

What are the triangles in *The Glass Menagerie*? Notice that for a long time, there are only three people in the play, so that Williams is constantly reshuffling alliances and relationships between Tom, Laura, and Amanda. Sometimes Tom and Laura are allied against Amanda, sometimes Tom and Amanda are allied against Laura, and—especially at the end—Laura and Amanda are united, separate from Tom.

But what happens when Jim appears in the play? Notice how the triangles become more complicated and lead to an even wider variety of relationships and scenes. Here are some variations that I noticed. Do you see any others?

Amanda, Tom, and Jim: Amanda and Tom plot and talk about Jim when he's an offstage character.
Amanda, Laura, and Jim: Amanda prepares Laura for Jim's arrival.
Amanda, Jim, and Tom: Amanda and Jim tease Tom about the electric bill.
Laura, Jim, and Amanda: Laura and Jim know a truth, which they have to share with Amanda.
Tom, Jim, and Laura: Jim understands what Tom has done and why.

Some of these relationships become visible in scenes played out onstage, others become important plot devices driving the action, others are hinted at offstage; but all of them interweave to make an interesting series of moments that connect with each other.

Why Today?

Dramas are typically about the unusual; characters thrown out of their normal lives (out of a state of equilibrium) and forced to cope with extraordinary circumstances. A good way to ensure that your play does this is to ask of the play, "Why today?" That is, what is unusual about *now* that makes a difference? What is happening *today* that is indeed extraordinary? Very often, the occasion has provoked the play's inciting incident, and its importance is one reason the stakes are so high.

Is today a special occasion? Plays often take place on birthdays, anniversaries, family gatherings, funerals, holidays, and so on. A list of some titles includes:

- *The Birthday Party* by Harold Pinter
- *The Long Christmas Dinner* by Thornton Wilder
- *August: Osage County* by Tracy Letts (a funeral)
- *Picnic* by William Inge (the small town's annual event)
- *The Rose Tattoo* by Tennessee Williams (the anniversary of a spouse's death)

Is something important happening today? The central action of *You Can't Take It with You* by Kaufman and Hart takes place on the night one set of future in-laws comes to dinner with the other. *Long Day's Journey into Night* occurs on the day Edmund finds out once and for all he does have tuberculosis. In *The Matchmaker* by Thornton Wilder, Barnaby and Cornelius have decided to take the day off, run to New York, and have an adventure. In Arthur Miller's *Death of a Salesman,* today is a double-hitter: not only has errant son Biff come home to visit, but Willie has made up his mind finally to ask his boss to take him off the road. And certainly we can't forget Jim's visit in *The Glass Menagerie.*

Nearly all classic Greek dramas take place on this one fatal day: Oedipus learns the truth, Agamemnon comes home, Medea is banished, Theseus's appearance proves he's not dead after all, and so forth. What's the special event in *Othello?*

Has somebody unexpected shown up? Blanche's arrival in *Streetcar Named Desire,* Hal's arrival *in Picnic,* the new employee in Joe Orton's *Entertaining Mr. Sloan* all provide examples of this device.

The Turnabout

If you recall our discussion of the well-made play's Freytag pyramid, you'll remember that two things often happen during the play's climax: there's a *reversal* and a *recognition*. Something is discovered that causes a change in somebody's fortune, or a violent change takes place that makes somebody realize a new thing. Often, the recognition is that somebody important is *not* the person we (or the agent of action) took them to be. We didn't know Dad was an alcoholic, cleverly covering his bases. We didn't realize that Mom was having an affair with a neighbor. We are amazed and overwhelmed when Uncle Billy is discovered to have embezzled a small fortune from his company. This sort of exposure plays pivotal roles in such plays as *A Streetcar Named Desire* (Blanche has a sordid secret past, which Stanley discovers), *Oedipus* (Oedipus himself is the murderer we seek), or Arthur Miller's *A View from the Bridge* (the father, Eddie Carbone, has long harbored incestuous feelings toward his niece).

There are two tricks to keep in mind with this device: *preparation* and *revelation*.

Preparing for the Turnabout

The first is to plant seeds throughout the early parts of the play, which upon first hearing seem innocent enough, but—upon reflection—can be seen for the clues they truly are. To set this up for yourself, sometimes it's useful (and fun) to create a chart of clues. One column might be labeled "Behaviors" and another might be called "Excuses." In the first, jot down all the behaviors that seem so normal, and in the other—corresponding—a seemingly plausible explanation, which, upon reflection, can be seen as another clue. Or to put it another way, column A is "He seems so normal," while column B is "But on the other hand . . ."

For instance, let's say the secret that's revealed is that Dad has secretly been embezzling funds from his company, where he works as an accountant. Your chart might look like this:

NORMAL BEHAVIOR	ON THE OTHER HAND . . .
Dad has a good middle-management job and makes a good salary.	Dad buys a new car every year, claiming that it saves money in the long run.

Dad is a dedicated employee.	Dad never misses a day, even when he's sick.
Dad is offered a promotion.	Dad has turned it down, claiming he likes it where he is.
Dad keeps within a careful budget.	Dad says he bets on horse races and uses his winnings to buy extravagant gifts.
Dad is typically a very friendly guy.	Dad treats a new co-worker with irrational hostility.
Dad is confident and easy-going.	Dad is very nervous about the five-year audit coming up.

You now can use the columns of your chart to create scenes that reveal those attributes, keeping in mind the principles of the Pigeon Sister and the exposition pig. You might create some scenes like these:

- Dad taking Mom along with him to talk to his favorite car dealer and trying to convince her that they can indeed afford that SUV for the trips they always dreamed of taking.
- Dad insisting he must go to work today, minimizing the seriousness of his flu symptoms and high fever.
- Dad, with his boss, turning down the new promotion and making up very good reasons.
- Dad presenting Mom with a rather large piece of jewelry for their anniversary.
- Dad making an enemy of the new employee.

Then, within the scope of your other elements (goal, obstacles, strategies, miniplays, etc.), fold these scenes into the overall fabric of the piece.

Here's how Eugene O'Neill does it in *Long Day's Journey into Night,* wherein the secret is Mary Tyrone's resuming her morphine habit.

NORMAL BEHAVIOR	ON THE OTHER HAND . . .
Mary is tense over Edmund's persistent cold.	She is nervous and fidgety.

Mary complains about Tyrone's snoring.	She has started sleeping alone again.
Mary complains excessively that people are spying on her.	She confronts the three other characters, forcing them to deny their suspicions, even going so far as to say, "It would serve you all right if it were true!"
Mary has to drive into town for some things.	The maid who accompanies her describes her strange behavior.
Mary stops caring.	She withdraws more and more into her past memories.

Keeping this chart in mind, go through that long play when you can and take note how and where O'Neill prepares us for the climax.

Revealing the Turnabout

The second trick to using this device is to be sure to make plausible the *reason* for the truth to come out. What happens that finally reveals to us Dad's secret crime? Does the auditor discover some obscure fact? Does Dad suffer a losing streak at the track and have to confess? Does Dad get laid off because of a recession?

What happens that gradually reveals Mary's secret? O'Neill sprinkles these moments throughout the play: each of the three men shows his suspicions, driving her deeper and deeper into her fears and paranoia and triggering her ever-growing need for more sedation.

Exercise 11:2

Try this for yourself in *The Glass Menagerie*. Let's agree for now that the big secret in the play is that Tom plans on escaping. While he makes no effort to disguise his unhappiness, we are still surprised that Tom actually abandons his mother and sister just when they need him most. On the other hand, Williams has sprinkled clues throughout the play. What are they? (Here's a hint to get you started: What has happened to the electric bill?)

Revision Questions

At any time in the writing of your play, you will surely find moments that are confusing to the audience: Where is the play going? Or moments that are dull and talky: Where is all this conversation going? Or that are digressive and wandering: How does this scene or this conversation help drive us to the climax? Or that are unsatisfying: The reversal seems too writerly and implausible. And so forth. Apply any one—or all four—of these "tricks" to help clarify for yourself what you're trying to do, or to help determine what to cut and what to revise.

12

Characterization

Earlier, when we spoke about *plot*, we looked briefly at the six elements Aristotle attributed to good drama. Plot, of course, came in first. Second is *character*—the depiction of more or less real people, about whom we often use the term *lifelike*, which is to say we expect them to function like actual living people, have well-rounded personalities, and operate according to some laws of logic and psychology. This is already a trap, isn't it?

In the first place, is this really what you're doing? Are the "characters" in *Everyman* supposed to be real people—labeled as they are by such titles as "Good-Deeds," "Fellowship," and "Beauty"? What about the "characters" in *The Adding Machine,* who are labeled "Mrs. Zero," "Mrs. One," "Mrs. Two," and so on? By no means are these meant to be the folks who live next door.

And even if they were the folks next door, who is to say what they are likely or not likely to do? When people say, "I don't believe Sally would do that," by what standards of behavior are they making that judgment? What does it mean to say, "Sally wouldn't do that"? I just showed you that she *did!*

And even if people were willing to accept your character's aberrant behavior, who is to say what makes a person "interesting" or "well-rounded"? While you may not find two people sitting in a room talking about the evils of capitalism and the value of free-trade for the third world nations to be fascinating, the person sitting next to you might find that fascinating beyond words. In plays like *Major Barbara, Man and Superman,* or *Heartbreak House,* George Bernard Shaw has his characters do exactly that.

Assumptions about Characters

The truth is that audiences expect characters in plays to behave in some ways that appear to be "real"; that is, real enough for us to believe, at least for the duration of the play, that such a person *might* actually live or have lived. They make the following assumptions about people, and if enough of these expectations are met, they'll accept what they see.

Characters Are Supposed to Be Consistent Throughout

That is, if you establish early that Jane is scared of fire, you can't have her lighting the campfire in act 3, unless one of the qp's was "Will Jane Overcome Her Irrational Fear of Fire?" Critics often find the scene in *The Glass Menagerie* of Jim getting Laura to dance to be "out of character" for Laura. But why? She does.

Characters Are Supposed to Operate according to Realistic Psychological Premises

In other words, their "motives" are supposed to be rational and understandable. This is the whole purpose of the first act of *Othello*: to show us that Othello is the kind of man who would murder his wife. We see him making hasty command decisions; we see him getting furiously angry; we see his puppylike devotion to his wife. Some people find *Othello* flawed in just this category. Why, they wonder, would a man who has risen in the ranks, spent intimate time with Iago, seen him operate with other people—why would such a man ever fall for so obvious a trick in the first place? A good question—but Shakespeare never bothers to deal with it. Does it hurt the play?

Characters Are Supposed to Be Multidimensional

We in the audience are supposed to see many different facets of a character's personality, even within a small, limited scope. Williams does this with all three Wingfields: Amanda is filled with illusions, but she does work hard in real life by selling magazine subscriptions. Laura is shy, but she does dance with Jim. Tom is a selfish dreamer, but he does bring home a gentleman caller.

Characters Are Supposed to Be Fluid

At the same time they're supposed to be consistent, characters are also supposed to somehow *change* as a result of the play's action. They're supposed to learn their lesson, reform, change their bad ways to good, suffer their well-deserved punishment, or what not. Aristotle's concept of the complex plot, with reversals and recognitions, depends on this assumption. And does Tom change: he gets out. But neither Amanda nor Laura change—except that Laura does "blow out" her candles. Othello changes: he kills himself. But Iago doesn't—except that he shuts up and never says another word.

Given these assumptions—that your characters are supposed to be consistent, interesting, psychologically accurate, and fluid— how do you do this?

How Much Do We Need to Know?

Before we get into *how* to reveal character, we need to address this prior question: *what* exactly are we trying to reveal? If we need to show many sides of a character, how many sides is that? Do we need to know everything about this person's life before the play, outside the play, after the play? Ibsen supposedly wrote lengthy biographies of his characters before he began to write them. Should you do the same? You'll find two opposing schools of thought about this.

The More the Merrier

Many teachers of writing often stress that, before you can write about your characters, you need to know all there is to know about them. These teachers advocate a large amount of advance thinking and preparation; they advise you to write extensive biographies of your people, making sure you include their child-hood, significant moments in their teenage years, what traumatic crises shaped their lives, how they got to the place in their lives when the curtain goes up, and other data.

I suppose the thinking behind such advice is that, once you know so much about your characters, you will subconsciously discover that these elements and facts will somehow find their way onto the page and your character will emerge fully finished. Or that, by inventing moments and important encounters of the past, you will discover scenes and lines of dialogue that you can somehow paste into your play.

Less Is More

However, I often see the downside in such advice. Often you trap yourself by knowing too much. After all, what good is it to know that Billy was scared by a spider at the age of six, unless that fact is important enough to find its way into the play? Because when it comes down to what the audience knows, nothing about your characters' lives before the play begins is important at all unless it is somehow important to the *present* action that is your play. What difference does the spider bite make to Billy now?

So there might indeed be some value in this extensive preparation. However, be careful to know exactly what you are doing here: that is, you may be spending a great of time writing your biographies because you're reluctant or unable to actually work on the play itself. Perhaps you're stuck, perhaps you're devoid of ideas, or perhaps you have a case of writer's anxiety—that little fear that what you're going to sit down and write just won't be good enough. In this case, writing biographies is busy work and can be useful just to keep you going.

Even so, you may find yourself placing too much importance on this biography. You've written something interesting that you're now reluctant to get rid of. It seemed vitally important when you thought of it, that Billy's arachnophobia be foregrounded, and so you find yourself twisting the plot around and inventing scenes just so you can bring this little tidbit in. A pretty clumsy cart going before an otherwise graceful horse.

Another reason I frown upon writing extensive biographies of your characters is that doing so really takes all the fun out of writing. I firmly believe that there ought to be a certain amount of surprise awaiting you when you sit down for your daily writing stint. Not being tied to some biographical formula allows you to invent what you need when you need it. If you need Billy to freak out on the day of his wedding, and you are looking for some psychological motive that would seem consistent with what else we know about Billy, *that* would be a good time to invent the spider. In other words, better to have the wedding and need the spider rather than have the spider and then need the wedding. Waiting until you need the device and inventing it on the spot will also make the spontaneous spider organic, the play will flow as you want it to, and you'll enjoy the surprise.

Therefore, taking both caveats into account, I encourage you to look for ways to enrich your characters, not by inventing a useless or inhibiting collection of facts about the past, but rather by looking at the kinds of things that happen in the present. These indicators can come from two sources: either inside the character, or from the outside.

Interior Indicators: Character through Action

Please recall one of the first points I made about characters in plays: audiences only know what they see and what they hear. The only real way to reveal anything at all about anybody is to put them in situations where their behavior objectively reveals who and what they are. That means that all characterization takes place in the present and is intimately bound to every other element of playwriting we've talked about. After all, if you've been reading carefully so far, you've noticed that I've managed to talk about character in almost every chapter of this book. Every aspect of your dramaturgy in some way always reveals some part of a person's character. There's a reason this chapter comes so late: consider it more a collection and review of good things you already know, rather than as new material.

How do you reveal character?

The Goal

What does your character want? If you remember, we looked at how an inner goal (such as "to be happy") needs to be translated into an outer, or story, goal. How will Bob know when he's happy? Remember HWHK? What does that concept mean to him objectively? That is, what has to happen in order for Bob to conclude he's where he wants to be?

Different people will, of course, have different answers to this question. So have you chosen your character's HWHK or HWSK wisely? Is "Getting an Oscar" really what Bob wants, or is his real goal to get Bill, who used to tease him miserably in high school, to finally say, "Boy, Bob; you're really cool"? Or is it, rather, his father finally shaking his hand and saying, "I'm proud of you"? Or is it his girlfriend finally saying, "Yes, I'll marry you," after all? Note how different each of these three goals is and what they say about Bob as a person.

Perhaps your play is about Bob seeking one goal, only to realize when he obtains it, that he really wants something else. Or perhaps you just don't know what his goal ought to be. In either case, try this.

Exercise 12:1

At the top of a blank sheet of paper, type: _____'s inner goal is to _____. Now type in ten different story goals that might lead to that. In other words, if Bob's inner goal is to find perfect happiness, his story goals might involve:

- getting an expensive foreign car;
- marrying Elizabeth;
- getting elected mayor;
- hearing his dad say, "I'm proud of you, son!";
- celebrating his one hundredth birthday

As you do, note for yourself what slight differences in your character's personality suggest themselves. Are any of these more accurate than what you have so far? Do any of these suggest nuances and shades of meaning that are relevant? If you suddenly write that Bob wants to buy a little red wagon—like the one he never had as a child—you've probably made an interesting discovery. Can you use it?

Obstacles

It has been said that you are known not only by the friends you keep but also by the enemies you make. It is the same for your characters. If, for instance, you want to somehow reveal that Gary, otherwise an upwardly mobile, super successful advertising man, is somehow flawed and vulnerable—after all, he has to have some flaws to make him sympathetic to Betty—you can think backwards. What would make him vulnerable? Say some irrational fear. Let's say, for now, it's fire. Review chapter 4; go down the list of sources of obstacles and invent five possible examples for each one and see what you learn about Gary. Now you need a way to put Gary into a situation where he faces fire, so that we can see this blemish and observe what he does about it.

Exercise 12:2

List five to ten situations: Gary is on a camping trip and has been put in charge of the fire; he's having dinner with Julie and a fire breaks out in the kitchen; he's being accused of embezzlement and needs to destroy evidence. What else? There are endless possibilities; see what you can learn. As you did with your character's goal, choose story elements that force the character into situations that reveal personality.

Strategies

And, of course, the exact same principle applies when it comes to creating the various strategies by which your character strives for success. In discussions in chapter 5, about both Amanda and Iago, we pointed out specific ways their choices of strategies illuminated their character for us.

Exercise 12:3

Try repeating the brainstorming exercise you did in chapter 5 (Exercise 5:3), this time applying your list of strategies to Gary. Jot down fifteen to twenty different strategies he might select that will enable him to get a fire lit, and see what each tells you. For example: He begs Steve to take his place; he pretends to faint; he tries to talk his companions out of the need for a fire; he calls on his magic powers to help; he kills everybody rather than reveal his cowardice. Be audacious. Let your imagination go wild. You may find some surprising ideas come to you that might well find their way into the play.

Hard Choices: The Squeeze

In his work on drama, *Poetics,* Aristotle defined *character* as that moment when somebody makes a moral choice, deciding which course of action to take at a crossroads. I have been alluding to this throughout the earlier parts of the book, suggesting that your character's choice of goals and strategies can be very revealing. Aristotle makes a similar point when he observes that a character is shown by what a man chooses or avoids.

You can emphasize this element by doing what I often call in my classes "The Squeeze." Again, it comes out of chapter 4 and is a simple technique that involves three basic steps:

- Early in the play, foreshadow that element which your character is most afraid of, most resistant to, or holds most at stake.
- Arrange events in the play so that your agent of action is faced with essentially a mutually exclusive choice—either to lose her goal or to achieve it only by facing her deadly fear. In other words, squeeze your character into a corner from which there is only one escape.
- Make the character choose.

In *The Glass Menagerie,* Tom is faced with a hard decision: either to stay in his family and continue to live the drab, suffocating life he has nightmares of, or to chuck it all, leave behind his mother and sister—that is, his responsibilities—and escape. His choice: he escapes. In *Othello,* Othello is faced with a hard decision: either to allow his wife to get away with cheating on him and thereby ruining his honor, or to kill her, even though he loves her desperately. His choice: He kills her. He's then faced with another hard decision five minutes later: to either live with the guilt of what he's done or take his own life. His choice: He kills himself. (Notice he doesn't kill Iago—what would *that* have said about him?)

How can we squeeze Gary into such a moment? Nobody volunteers to light the fire. His archenemy Victor has publicly dared him to strike the match, and everybody's watching. His girlfriend threatens to leave him right now unless . . . , and so on. You can do better.

The Torvald Moment

Refer back to chapter 11 where I introduced this concept. It comes directly upon the heels of The Squeeze. If you can actually conceive and write out that one line of dialogue that is most crucial to your character and find a way to bring it into a climactic moment, your audience will know more about your character than any lengthy scene or monologue can accomplish.

Exercise 12:4

Again, brainstorming can surprise and help you. Write down at random seven to ten lines of dialogue your character might reveal in a spontaneous outburst in a moment of stress. What can you learn? For instance, what is revealed about a person who says:

- But you're not really my son, are you?
- Okay, okay, eat the last piece of pizza, you pig!
- You never buy me anything I really want!
- I hate Thanksgiving, *especially* at your mother's house!
- What, you think I married you for your *looks?*

The Pigeon Sister

Do you remember what this tool involves? Creating some object or event that requires characters to act upon, to make decisions about, to create activities to accomplish, to do something. Our phrase came from *The Odd Couple,* wherein the Pigeon Sister plot device was played by the Pigeon sisters themselves, and we examined in some detail the climactic scene in *The Glass Menagerie* to note the difference between action and discussion. Gary's Pigeon Sister might be handling the fire starter: one of those self-contained butane lighters with the trigger and the long handle. Since Gary has never lit a fire, he's never had to use one. Victor tries to show him how, and Gary just becomes more and more frightened. Or have him building the fire itself—laying down the tinder and the twigs and the branches in precisely the right sequence.

Language Choices

A person's chosen vocabulary tells us a great deal about him or her; the words someone chooses to describe an object, achieve a goal, express a thought, and so forth, are really nothing more than an inner thought translated into an audible action. Consider Miss Muffet for a moment. What kind of woman does she seem to be when she uses each of these expressions?

- I have a terrible fear of spiders.
- Oooooooh, spiders are icky!
- I hate spiders! I would kill them all if I could.
- Those monsters are in the yard again!
- Spiders! Oh my lord, they scare the _____ out of me!

(You fill in the blank with whatever word you think she'd use, and then consider what kind of woman you have made her.)

A careful examination of the vocabularies in *The Glass Menagerie* will show you how carefully Williams has drawn his characters through their word choices. For example: Tom refers to "visitors"; Amanda calls them "gentleman callers." Tom calls Laura a "cripple"; Amanda insists she only has a "slight disability." What we learn is that Tom is a man who deals with the harsh realities of life, while Amanda continues to live in the dream world of her Southern past.

Other language choices might involve your answers to some of the following questions:

- Does your character use proper grammar or street slang?
- Does your character speak in coherent and often full sentences or in scattered fragments of words?
- Does your character speak directly to the point or waffle around the subject?

- Does your character swear a lot or hardly at all? What expletives does the character use, if any?
- Does your character have any sort of accent? Does the character sound like someone from New York City or Alabama or somewhere in between?
- What is the rhythm of your character's lines? Are they sharp and percussive or languid and flowing?

External Indicators

All of the elements we've been discussing so far in this chapter have been those that are intrinsic to the character: those internal thoughts, drives, and choices of the character, insofar as they are shown to us by various actions. But playwrights often overlook other factors—external ones—that can be very useful as well. Here are some tools available to you.

Foil Characters

A *foil* is a character who compares or contrasts with another character in the play. By recognizing or understanding what this person is like, we get to see what the other character is not like. Thus, we come to appreciate how noble and virtuous Othello is by noting how different he is from the evil and treacherous Iago. Likewise, Cassio becomes clearer to us by also being contrasted with Iago. Both men are concerned with their reputations, but Cassio takes an open and somewhat honest approach to being rehabilitated, while Iago sneaks around doing bad things in revenge. Contrast Desdemona herself with Iago: she can't understand the evil in the world, while Iago personifies it. Contrast Roderigo with Iago; contrast Brabantio with Iago; contrast Emilia with Iago—and you'll note how richly Shakespeare has drawn them by showing us loudly and plainly what they are *not* like.

Are there characters in your play with whom your agent of action interacts? In what way can you make them contrast with each other?

Are there characters already in your play who are almost foils but, with a little tweaking, can be more useful? Can the neighbor next door be a little more suspicious, while Sally is a little more trusting? Can the bank president be a little more perfunctory, while Bill is a little more patient?

Physical Traits

Insofar as possible, are there physical traits your character might have that reflect his or her inner state? It is always dangerous to write characters with this in mind, since you may not always be able to actually cast an actor of that physical type; but you can put as much on the page as you think will help.

Is there something important about the character's size? Several plays insist that the leading woman be large: O'Neill's *A Moon for the Misbegotten* and LaBute's *Fat Pig,* for instance. Other plays insist the female should be small and frail, as Williams does in *A Streetcar Named Desire.*

Is there a physical disability that matters? Laura has a bad leg. In the French farce *A Flea in Her Ear,* a main character has a speech impediment, as does the title character in *Billy Budd.* Is there something about the character's appearance? Does he wear his hair in a certain way because he's making a comment about the world, as do the angry young men in *Hair?* Does she sport a particular color of clothing because it reflects her personality? Does he still wear a full business suit, even on casual Friday?

You will find that questions like these often pop up during production meetings about your play. You will hear such questions from costume, scenic, and lighting designers, as well as directors. If Amanda is dressed in white, what colors should Tom and Laura wear to show how they contrast? If Amanda lives in a world of illusions, how has she decorated her apartment—are there old-fashioned lamps with shades or does she have wall fixtures? At the end of the play, when Amanda has been shaken out of her dream world, what color does the lighting now take? Is it more white and less pink?

While your play may not be in production at this time, it will still be immensely useful for you to envision and write into the text as much of this kind of material as you can—it all goes toward the total impression you want your character to make on the audience.

Physical Surroundings

What does the character surround herself with? How does she use these objects? What does the physical environment say about Laura, for instance? She lives in a flat with only two bedrooms. She lives with her mother and brother and her two primary toys. There's a fire escape, which is the only access, besides the front door, to the outside.

But beyond what is there, how does the character *use* these elements? How does she give them life and purpose? Notice that Laura spends nearly all her time onstage involved with her family, her phonograph records, and her glass animals. She tries to be a broker between Amanda and Tom; in times of crisis, she retreats to either the couch or the phonograph. She has to be forced to go to the front door. She has to be ordered to go the grocer's, and she hates it. The only time she's on the fire escape is when her mother makes a wish on the moon. We never see her going in the kitchen, clearing the table, sweeping the floor, answering the phone, reading the magazine her mother tries to sell, and so forth. In a sense, everything in her environment becomes either a Pigeon Sister or a possible source for one.

What Do Others Say about Them?

Amanda describes Laura as "special," and she tells Tom that Laura is "so quiet, but still waters run deep." She reminds him that "she just drifts along, doing nothing." She characterizes her daughter as a "dismal failure," and so forth. Notice how other people describe Othello: Iago calls him a fool, Roderigo insults his race, the Duke admires him, Desdemona is worried about his recklessness, and so forth. Suppose Gary were offstage for a few moments? What would Betty say to Victor that would tell us all we need to know about Gary?

What Do They Reveal about Themselves?

Some people love to talk about themselves; other people hate to. But there are always occasions when we talk about ourselves and reveal bits of our character. Often these are casual comments, but consider this: If you casually ask a person, "How are you feeling today?" what range of responses might you get? Some people will tell you they're okay and let it go. Others will describe their current physical ailment and move on. Still others might not even answer you at all. Different characters, all of them.

In moments of intimacy or bonding, people often express their fears, hopes, expectations, and reactions. Notice how much we learn about Jim in *The Glass Menagerie* even though he's only on-stage for fifteen minutes. Notice how often Amanda describes her past and how seldom Laura does. Notice how Othello describes his glorious military life and his wooing of Desdemona.

Of course, there's a catch to all this self-revelation: When does it work in the scene, and when does it appear as sloppy writing? In early plays, writers could get away with soliloquies or asides to the audience. Iago reveals himself fully to us by directly telling us what a villain he is and how he's going to destroy his boss. Hamlet does this constantly, as do Richard III and Henry V and dozens of others.

We, however, because soliloquies are no longer considered "realistic," have to make sure the revelation comes naturally in the context and does not appear forced. The solution lies, as it did in regard to exposition, in using the information as a *strategy*. Why does Jim say all those things about himself? To make Laura feel better. Why does Othello talk so much about his exploits? To convince the Duke that he is worthy of Desdemona.

Revision Questions

What kind of questions might you get that address characterization?

> I didn't believe she would steal the money.
> The character was just dull; I knew in five minutes all I needed to know.
> I didn't understand what his problem was.
> Nothing happened; it was all the same.
> There was just too much talk and not enough action.

Some questions to ask yourself include the following:

1. Have you chosen your agent's goal effectively? Have you translated an inner goal into an outer goal that is specific, clear, and obvious?

2. Have you selected the right obstacles to help reveal sides of the character's personality? Refer to chapter 4.

3. Review the strategies your agent pursues. Are they the most effective? If you were to brainstorm a list of ten to fifteen more, would you discover new and unusual ones that can work better?

4. Write what would be a "Torvald moment" line. It doesn't have to be actually written into the script—unless it works—but it can be useful for you to use as a guideline.

5. Does your character grow or change as a result of her actions? Is it clear that her personality has altered? That she has learned something, made important decisions, and so on?

6. Have you made the most effective use of external indicators: foils? Have you made the most effective use of other characters' descriptions, physical settings, Pigeon Sisters, and so on?

7. Have you carefully chosen the right language? How do your characters' word choices, use of language, and rhythm of speech all reveal character?

Epilogue: Revisions

You've probably heard the old cliché, and, you know, it's true: *Plays are not written: They are rewritten, over and over again.* Many new writers find this process daunting; they would like to think the first effort is *it*. Done, finished—a masterpiece. This is never the case, and there are several good reasons why.

Plays are not written to be read but to be performed. What is written on the page *never* presents the same way when the play is up on its feet and actors are delivering the lines, moving around, playing the moments. Dialogue that looks right when written may be awkward and difficult to speak. Scenes that seem at first to make sense come across to the audience as confusing, or too long, or not long enough for their points to be understood. You may have too many miniplays; you may not have enough. You may think an actor has time to make a quick costume change, but he in fact doesn't. You may have written something like "John goes offstage to get a glass of water and comes back upset"—only to realize that while John is offstage, *nothing* is happening onstage, and the actors are standing around waiting. In other words, countless little things that seem fine in your head or on the page simply do not come across in performance.

You may have written the wrong play. The play you started out with two months ago has somehow transformed itself into something completely different: a plot twist has sent the story into a new direction; a small character has somehow become a major one; somebody's goal or HWHK has become lost, confused, or changed; or it's only now, two months after you've finished, that you yourself suddenly come to know what your play is really about—it's not your grandmother's illness that's important, it's Sophie's reaction to it that counts. It's not Grandma's play at all; it's Sophie's. And when this happens, of course you have to go back to the beginning and all over the middle in order to change things to make them clearer.

You may just have written first-draft garbage after all. The play as it stands might be ultimately uninteresting, clumsy, boring, too long, too short, too much a cliché, or suffer from any number of possible shortcomings. This happens. It happens to every single writer I have ever met, studied, or worked with. There's just a certain amount of dross we all have to clear away to get down to the gold. Whatever the reason, chances are your first draft is not working. Do not panic. This is a good thing. You have to write and clear away the bad stuff before you can reach the good underneath.

The difficult thing at this point is to understand what to do next.

The first thing is to find out what you have. This means allowing other people to read your work and give you feedback. You may do this any number of ways. Invite a professional friend or colleague (your teacher?) to read the play and meet with you. Or gather some friends around your dining room table, pass out parts, and just read what you have. Or approach a theater and work with them to put together a public reading—casting the play with real actors, rehearsing it once, twice, or not at all, inviting people to come listen, and having a talkback afterwards. (This last is the best option if you can make it happen, for all the reasons discussed above why plays are different when performed than when read.)

And then you have to figure out what to fix.

How Do You Know What to Fix?

Your reading is over, you've had some feedback from others. And the reactions to the play are mixed. Some people praised certain parts; other people found fault with those same parts. Some people understood what you were trying to do; others had no clue. Some people liked your characters; others found one or more of them confusing or uninteresting. If you're like everybody else, you may be confused, disappointed, angry, or frustrated. We'll deal with this emotional freight in a moment.

But at any rate, you are extremely vulnerable. You're at a potentially dangerous time in your work on this play. I say this from experience, having gone through developmental steps numerous times with my own work as well as being a mentor and teacher to my students. I see this time and again: the response to a play, if it's not understood and treated properly, is like a germ-ridden disease; it can often kill what the writer is trying to do. Because of the responses, you're tempted to cut out a character who "isn't working," add scenes that make the play more "active," or "exciting," reshuffle relationships among characters, rearrange scenes, add more laughs, cut out too many laughs, change the curtain line, or worse—throw it all out and start over again with a different idea.

Now, I'm not saying these are invalid reactions. You may, after some consideration, come to the same conclusions yourself. But it's the "after some consideration" part that concerns us here. Then how do you know what to fix? Whom do you listen to, and how do you decide what to do?

The answers to these questions, of course, always depend on you, your play, where you are in its total development process, and what basically you are trying to do. Therefore, rather than give you specific steps to follow, let me suggest some serious questions you must ask yourself at this point. Only you can answer them.

Be Honest and Ask Yourself Whether or Not You Really Want Feedback

Sometimes when you finish a first draft, you still don't know what the play is about; there are still many unsolved problems and unanswered questions. Perhaps at this stage, all you want is praise and credit for a job well done. There's nothing wrong with this—we all want to be nicely stroked—but if that's the case, don't ask for opinions or reactions because you may not really be ready to hear them. It takes some distance and a great deal of objectivity to listen to critical feedback. If you don't hear the praise you want, you'll only wind up being hurt and disappointed, angry at your responder, and blocked from any other useful thoughts that might come to you.

What Do You Want to Learn from the Feedback You Are Going to Get?

Hopefully, at this point you have some ideas about what problems you're facing and where this draft might be weakest. Are you still trying to stumble on what the play is about? That might take several drafts. Are you concerned that the person you think is the agent of action might be overshadowed by another character, who might make it a more interesting play? Are you worried about fat, dull exposition? Laughs? Are there specific moments in the play that you aren't sure are clear, compelling, or tight enough?

It's very useful to let your responders know up-front—even before they read the play sometimes—exactly what you are looking for. This advance knowledge helps them focus their attention as they read (or watch); it also helps direct their comments to areas that are most useful to you. When I host public discussions of my students' work, I always preface the evening with a list of these pertinent questions.

What Areas of the Play Do You Not Want to Talk About?

There may be ideas or scenes or characters still unfinished in your head. You may still be trying to sort out for yourself what these things will become. Or you may be dealing with very personal material and not feel that, at this stage in your work, you can be objective enough to take criticism. Or you may have already made your mind up about some cuts and don't want to waste time talking about dead-issue things. Whatever the reason, it's perfectly fine for you to set limits to what you might hear.

How? When you ask for feedback, simply say to your responder, "Let me tell you in advance that I'm not ready to talk about Daisy's suicide just yet. I'm still working on it, and whatever you say might throw me off track. Same with Johnny's coming out process; that's still unfinished in my head."

Are Your Critics Reliable?

Everybody who reads or hears your play will have a different agenda and use a different lens. Your mother will think it's brilliant. Actors in your reading will look at the play from the perspective of the characters they play. Lay audience members will often want to show off how smart they are by offering you suggestions on how to rewrite the play. Writers will give you thoughts as writers and directors as directors. Nobody is objective, even though they may appear to be.

Of course, these are overgeneralizations; it's wrong to prejudge any response you get. But be aware: The more theatrically expert your responders are, the more likely their responses might be useful. Having said this, however, let me urge you to pay close attention to the two following questions:

If you have sat through a public reading before an audience, what have you learned from the audience during the reading itself? It's an old adage in the theater: people in the audience aren't always right, but an audience, as an audience, is hardly ever wrong. Collectively, as people watch the play, they have unified responses. What is funny will make everybody laugh, or at least smile. What is tense and compelling will make everybody sit still, lean forward, and pay quiet and close attention. What is dull and boring will make everyone shuffle in their seats, rattle their programs, or yawn noisily. If you sit in the audience, you'll be in the middle of these reactions and feel firsthand just how the crowd is experiencing your play. You'll know when the moments in the play aren't doing their job.

Afterward, at the talkback session, if there is one, you might ask questions that refer to those moments. If you ask, "What moments seemed to bore you the most?" and everybody nods when the young man in the back row says, "Every one that involved Steve; he was useless," you pretty much have to accept the fact that Steve might be your first casualty.

What comments are you consistently hearing from a variety of responders? If the majority of people you ask offer you a similar answer, you are wise to believe in what they say. If three out of every four think the climax is weak, look carefully at your climax. Listen for consistent reactions to similar things and use them as guideposts.

After you've collected all your responses, what's the best thing to do next? This depends a great deal on you, your writing habits, your objectivity, and numerous other factors. You may be a little shaken and confused; if so, put the play away for a period of time and let it simmer in your head until you feel ready to tackle the problems. Or you may have heard some very inspiring and stimulating comments and be ready to go right back to work; if so, do so.

But whenever you do get back into the saddle again, do not try to tackle all the problems at once; just as you did not have to have a perfect first draft, you do not have to have a perfect second one either. Take each major area at a time and let the new draft focus on it. Let the second draft be about plot; the next be about character; the next be about dialogue.

Dealing with Emotional Freight

As I suggested earlier, you may experience strong emotional reactions to the responses you get. This is unavoidable; even the most professional and experienced writers I know admit that they feel vulnerable when their first drafts are exposed. Why not? You've invested a great deal of time and energy, not to mention blood, sweat, and tears, in creating this hopefully living thing. A great deal of it has come from deep, personal reservoirs of your heart and soul. You have expectations and hopes. And you want to know that the effort has been worth it. Therefore, when people tell you it's flawed, your first reaction is bound to be one of some disappointment. How do you handle it? How do you avoid it?

You don't avoid it, but you recognize it for what it is. It's a natural human response. Okay. You're hurt; you're mad. You're the worst writer in the world. You're useless as a human being and ought to be extinguished like a candle. You're all of these things and more. Okay. You've felt this way before; you'll feel this way again. Take a deep breath. And get over it. Realize the emotional noise for what it is. And then put it aside and look objectively at what you now have to do in order to make the flawed play brilliant.

This process takes time. For some of us, it might take minutes; for others a few hours; for others—most of us, if we're honest—a day or so. This is one reason I am personally not in favor of those immediate open discussions that often have to accompany public readings of new works. You just need time to regain your objectivity, and you don't always have it. If this is the case, you simply have to force yourself to listen very hard and put away the emotional stuff until you can deal with it later. Take copious notes; it will give you something to do. Look at them later and try to sort out the relevant ones from the nonsense.

Again, let the process take time. Allow yourself to be a human being. After all, isn't that what makes you a great writer?

Glossary
Index

Glossary

Agent of Action. One of the functions a character might fulfill and often called the protagonist, this is the character who has a main goal in the play and whose efforts to achieve this goal drive the action forward; that is, the character who "makes things happen."

Character. One of the six elements that Aristotle lists as the components of an overall dramatic action and that refers to the people who inhabit the play.

Character-driven. Describes a play in which the interest lies more in the revelation of character than it does in the unfolding of the plot.

Climax. The point in a well-made play at which the story turns in a major new direction and the agent of action faces a final obstacle and often makes final choices. The climax may contain a reversal and/or a recognition.

Complex Plot. An Aristotelian term that refers to a plot in which a character undergoes both a reversal and a recognition.

Crisis. A moment in the play in which a character is faced with a new development or unexpected problem (an obstacle) and must undertake a new strategy.

Exposition. Any information that the audience is given that helps them understand the background of the play, the previous lives of the characters, or some event that has happened offstage.

Failed Strategy. A character's scheme to achieve his or her goal which fails, causing the character to abandon that scheme and try another.

Foil. One of the functions a character might fulfill, this is any person who in some way compares or contrasts with another and who is used to illuminate the personality of other characters as well as to help dramatize the meaning of the play.

HWHK. Abbreviation for "How Will He Know?" This phrase refers to the external, physical event that needs to occur in order for a character to know he has achieved the goal he set out for himself; it involves translating an inner, psychological need to an outer manifestation.

HWSK. Abbreviation for "How Will She Know?" *See* HWHK.

Inciting Incident. The second step of a well-made play, this refers to that disturbance of the state of equilibrium by a person or event that forces the agent of action to begin to take steps to achieve a goal.

Language. One of the six elements that Aristotle lists as the components of an overall dramatic action, this refers to the choice of words the characters use to communicate.

Major Dramatic Question (MDQ). That central question that runs through the whole play, causing the audience to wonder whether or not the agent of action will achieve his or her goal. It appears in a well-made play as a result of the inciting incident having disturbed the state of equilibrium.

Major Question of Plot (QP). A long-range, major dramatic question, one that runs through the length of the play.

miniplay. A section of a well-made play that, in itself, contains the four necessary ingredients that make up the core of such a play, that may be as short as one or two lines, or that may contain several smaller miniplays, operating like a set of nesting dolls inside each other.

minor question of plot (qp). An immediate, short-term, here-and-now dramatic question.

Music. One of the six elements that Aristotle lists as essential to a well-made play, this refers to the audible component of the performance, including music, speech, or the euphonics of the language.

Overall Dramatic Action. The essential thing that a play tries to show, a specific event that occurs over a limited time in which a significant change occurs.

Pigeon Sister. A plot device, named after characters in Neil Simon's *The Odd Couple*, that provides the substance or excuse for characters to engage in some action.

Plot. One of the six elements that Aristotle lists as the components of an overall dramatic action, this refers to the selection and arrangement of the incidents, or how the story is told.

Presentational. Describes a form of drama in which the actors break the "fourth wall" and interface directly with the audience, as does the Stage Manager in Thornton Wilder's *Our Town*.

Question of Character (QC). One of the key forms of the dramatic questions that raise and sustain an audience's interest; this one usually appears after the climax of a play, when the Major Dramatic Question has been answered, and deals with changes in the personality of the character involved.

Question of Information (QI). One of the key forms of dramatic questions that raise and sustain an audience's interest, this one involves the *who, what, where, how,* and so on of the characters and events of the play and typically has a fact for an answer.

Recognition. Something that a character comes to understand or learn as a result of the events of the play. Often considered part of a complex plot.

Resolution. Those events in a well-made play that occur after the climax and that typically show how the play now moves to a new state of equilibrium; often called the *falling action*.

Reversal. A moment in a play in which a character's fortunes shift, when something happens to change the circumstances and turn the story in a new direction. Often considered part of a complex plot.

Rising Action. The central part of a well-made play dealing with those events and strategies that occur as the agent of action tries to achieve his or her goal. It consists of a series of crises that gradually build tension as they move toward the climax.

Side Strategy. An attempt or scheme that a character undertakes temporarily to achieve his or her goal, often because a main strategy is suspended or blocked for some reason.

Spectacle. One of the six elements that Aristotle lists as the components of an overall dramatic action, this refers to the visual impact made by the production. While it may reflect the ideas in the play, it is not necessarily part of the text.

Squeeze. A plot device in which a character is forced by a set of circumstances to make a crucial decision with limited, mutually exclusive options.

State of Equilibrium. One of the seven steps of a well-made play, this shows us what the world is like, how it is stable, before it is interrupted by an inciting incident.

Substrategy. An interim attempt or scheme that a character undertakes as an incremental step in carrying out a larger strategy. Sometimes a well-made play involves a complicated nesting of substrategies within substrategies.

Thought. One of the six elements that Aristotle lists as the components of an overall dramatic action, this refers to the ideas that the characters express through language.

Torvald Moment. A plot device in which a character utters a spontaneous, unplanned remark, most often in the heat of the moment, that reveals an important truth about himself or herself, or about someone else, and which is named after such a moment in Ibsen's *A Doll's House.*

Triangles. A plot device in a well-made play that occurs when three characters are involved in a complex relationship with shifting alliances and negotiations.

Turnabout. A plot device in a well-made play wherein something or someone suddenly reveals the hidden side of a character in a new and often striking light. Using this device effectively involves careful foreshadowing.

Well-Made Play. Originally (in the nineteenth century) a play written according to a particular formula, it now refers to any play that is structured according to a specific pattern of events and that attempts to show a realistic world behaving in a logical cause-and-effect fashion.

Index

action, 4, 6, 68, 92, 93; Aristotle on, 63–64; characterization and, 113–14; contrasts and, 67–68; conversation versus, 119–20; *The Glass Menagerie* and, 66–68, 114–20; language as, 149; list of strategies and, 53; overall dramatic, 16, 65, 66; and questions of plot, 90, 166; past as motive for, 123; Pigeon Sister and, 110–11, 112, 114–20; and questions of plot, 90; rising, 70, 73–74, 76, 77, 167; and understanding characters, 67

actors, 5, 8, 36, 78, 155, 159

advanced tricks, in playwriting, 4–5, 109–54

agent of action, 25–27, 28, 44; versus central character, 26–27; defined, 165; in five-minute play, 46; in *The Glass Menagerie*, 27, 72; goal of, 31; and inciting incident, 69; and questions of character, 93; and rising action, 70. *See also* character; protagonist

Amanda Wingfield (*The Glass Menagerie*), as agent of action, 27

anticipation, and dramatic questions, 87–88

appearance, physical, and characterization, 151

arc of play, 18

argument, 112–14

Aristotle, 166, 167; on character, 140, 142, 147, 165; on climax, 75; on key ingredients of plays, 64–65; on plays, 61–65; on plot, 65

arrangement of incidents, 65, 68–71, 166; and Freytag pyramid, 69–76; linear versus nonlinear, 69

Art of Fiction, The (Henry James), 13

asides, and characterization, 153

assistance, as obstacle, 43

audience, 5, 31, 55; and exposition, 121; feedback during play, 159; writing for, 6, 20

Backwards and Forwards: A Technical Manual for Reading Plays (Ball), 53

Bald Soprano, The (Ionesco), 69

beginner, playwright as, 8–9

behavior. *See* goal, inner and outer

Betrayal (Pinter), 69, 76

biographies, of characters, 142–44

bond with another, as reason for exposition, 126, 153

brick house, play as, 79

building blocks, fundamentals of drama as, 4, 6, 61, 65, 87

Castagno, Paul, 8

causal order, and arrangement of incidents in play, 14, 68, 69

cautions, for beginning playwright, 5–9

change, 15, 17–18, 94; within characters, 142; conveyed by physical act, 31; and exposition, 124; of fortune, 63; four levels of, 21–22; major, 76; on multiple levels, 20; and question of character, 93; in realistic plays, 123–24; types of, 18–20

David Rush is a professor and head of playwriting in the Department of Theater at Southern Illinois University Carbondale. He is the author of *A Student Guide to Play Analysis*, adopted as a text by universities across the country, and was named Playwriting Teacher of the Year in 2002 by the Association for Theatre in Higher Education. His plays have been produced in Los Angeles, New York, and Chicago, and other productions and readings of his plays have been done by the Utah Shakespeare Festival, the Orlando Harriet Lake New Plays Festival, the William Inge Residency, the Great Plains Theater Conference, and other national workshops. His work has received two Emmys and three Jeff Awards as well as the Los Angeles Dramalogue Award for Excellence. Formerly a Resident Writer of Chicago Dramatists, he is also a member of Chicago's Stage Left Theatre Company.